TREASURE WITHIN

A Memoir

by

Meryl M Williams

Other works by the same author

<u>Poetry with photographs</u>
Moods in Bloom

<u>Short Stories</u>
Andrew's Amazing Odyssey and other stories

<u>Novellas</u>
The Judge Jones Trilogy
My Lady's Sovereign
Mortymer House

THE AUTHOR - MERYL M WILLIAMS
Born 1966

Meryl was born in South Wales and studied bio-medical sciences in Cardiff then worked for a time in London, Bath and Texas USA. On returning to Bath, England, she settled on writing first poetry, then prose. Her work is inspired by people she meets, places she visits and the unfailing appeal of the Natural World.

In this semi-autobiographical work she focuses on faith, the universal wisdom that people have expressed throughout the generations and how to survive in a positive way.

Quotes from Good News Bible, edition 2017.

TREASURE WITHIN PART 1
CONTENTS

The Road Not Taken
Robert Frost (1874 - 1936)

Two roads diverged in a yellow wood,
And sorry I could not travel both
And be one traveller, long I stood
And looked down one as far as I could
To where it bent in the undergrowth;

Then took the other, as just as fair,
And having perhaps the better claim,
Because it was grassy and wanted wear;
Though as for that the passing there
Had worn them really about the same,

And both that morning equally lay
In leaves no step had trodden black.
Oh, I kept the first for another day!
Yet knowing how way leads on to way,
I doubted if I should ever come back.

I shall be telling this with a sigh
Somewhere ages and ages hence:
Two roads diverged in a wood, and I -
I took the one less travelled by,
And that has made all the difference.

I.

UPSKILL IN DIVERSITY

Episode 1 - Completely Filled.

Ephesians 3: 18, 19
So that you, together with all God's people, may have the power to understand how broad and long, how high and deep, is Christ's love. Yes, may you come to know his love - although it can never be fully known - and so be completely filled with the very nature of God.

I remember just a few years ago, being invited to enter a competition. We were asked to write, draw or create a piece of craft that told the story of a woman that had inspired us. I wrote about a one time very public figure but as I write today I am thinking of Her Majesty Queen Elizabeth I and the threat of the Spanish Armada in 1588.

Before the days of fast cars, newspapers and the Internet, the Queen sat on her horse as she made the speech of her career. She spoke resoundingly as she said
"Though I have the mind and body of a woman, yet I have the heart and spirit of a King and a King of England too". It's said that the Spanish ships were big and cumbersome whereas the fleet of smaller English vessels could cut in underneath the Spanish guns to cause the invading ships to sink. England resisted invasion and has done so since the days of the Norman Conquest of 1066.

Moving across the pond, in 1863 Abraham Lincoln, then President of the United States of America, wrote his famous Gettysburg address. The speech was for the dedication of the Soldiers National Cemetery at Gettysburg, Pennsylvania. Union armies had defeated Confederate forces in the Battle of Gettysburg so in his speech, the President refers to the "four score years and seven" that had passed since the Declaration of Independence 87 years before.

While Lincoln paid his respects to the war dead of that conflict he said, "it is for us the living, rather, to be dedicated here to the unfinished work which they who fought here have thus far so nobly advanced".

Legend has it that Lincoln wrote this time honoured address on the back of an old envelope when on the train but it is also said that this was unlikely as his speeches were well planned and polished.

A journey of faith will have many peaks and troughs. I am old enough to remember the Troubles of Northern Ireland although we hardly hear it mentioned now. It was my first year of College in Cardiff in 1984 and I was lodging with a really lovely older couple. The gentleman explained that they very rarely had the television on over breakfast but they made an exception as the news had just been announced about the Conservative party conference hotel being bombed. It's something they always say in America isn't it? "Do you remember where you were when President Kennedy was shot?" I am too young for that incident but somehow it's the disasters and the negative incidents that we focus on as a society especially with respect to our always gloomy news. But the sun is shining as I write this and it's much easier to be positive at such a time.

At the front of this book I typed a very enjoyable poem about a choice of roads and the perennial, very human dilemma as to which route should I take? Also what if?

Aslan in "The Lion, the Witch and the Wardrobe", says "no one is ever told what would have happened". Looking at that intriguing poem by Robert Frost it's the last line I love the best. Two choices of route, two very different outcomes so here on in is my big opportunity to reflect on paths I have taken, choices I have made and the decisions that led me to write, to get published and finally in book ten to speak to my readers today.

Episode 2 - The Certainty of Change

Psalm 103 : v11-13
*As high as the sky is above the earth,
so great is his love for those who honour him.
As far as the east is from the west,
so far does he remove our sins from us.
As a father is kind to his children,
so the Lord is kind to those who honour him.*

Change can be a mixed blessing to the extent that some alteration to the status quo may be necessary but sometimes we can be left feeling that there are changes that are only virtuous because they are different. Some people advocate that change should be resisted at all costs but we know that many changes have come into force in recent years whereas our ethics, living standards or way of life maintains a basic pattern of freedoms that we enjoy but at terrible cost to those that went before. Every Remembrance Day we hear the same rhetoric about the glorious dead who made the ultimate sacrifice that we might be free and every year yet more die in the same fruitless pursuit. If they could speak to us now how would they advise us?

But we have no fear, because one death was sufficient to erase the mistakes of the past, one sacrifice in the crucifixion and resurrection of Jesus Christ overpowers death and sets us free. That is our living hope which keeps us focussed on a higher power and perfect solution.

Probably the biggest change I saw in my own experience was a relocation across the pond to a more senior position in an American University. It was an opportunity I would have been silly to pass by and I am still really glad to this day that I got there. It was challenging, stressful and difficult. I was very homesick, found that driving everywhere when I infinitely preferred to walk was detrimental to my well being and am even more inclined to rejoice that I made it back home to my long suffering family as they still remain the prop and mainstay of my support.

But while I was in Texas I joined a church choir and what an amazing, lovely, never to be missed time that was. We processed in red robes with crosses around our necks and sang to a band in the church gallery. It's a discipline although now I am middle aged my voice is rather ropey and croaky but they say that singing is very good for one's health. Coming home from America I had to reinvent my own life, rethink my whole existence and make radical changes as my time as a high flying academic had come to an abrupt close.

At 12.45am on 15th April 1912 RMS Titanic made its first wireless call for assistance. Later it used the code SOS which was its first use by a passenger liner. When the luxury cruise ship was built in Belfast she was thought to be practically unsinkable but foundered after striking ice on her maiden voyage at 2.20am after that distress call. There were insufficient lifeboats for everyone on board and the first of these was picked up at 4.10am which was a long delay in open boats on icy seas. RMS stands for Royal Mail Ship and the huge hulk was intended to carry post as well as a cargo of coal and of course passengers.

I have to admit, with hindsight which is a wonderful thing, that when I achieved my doctorate in the late summer of 1992 I thought I was practically unsinkable. My faith was fairly new and my career was the business of my life. I have heard it said that it is well to be mindful of being over-obsessed with one thing in case you lose it and the last thing

I really expected was a diagnosis of bipolar and to give all of that up.

I had previously had a friend who passed his Grade 8 exam on the piano which I said was the end as the system goes no higher. He said that it was in fact the beginning, a very positive way of seeing an important landmark. As I write this segment of my book, it's a frosty morning and the news is all about climate change and an agreement to support poorer nations who are the worst affected. This is indeed the beginning even though all the finer details have not yet been thrashed out.

Yesterday (19th November 2022) I walked through beautiful, local woodlands to visit the American Museum in Bath (pictured at night), in my near neighbourhood. On the way I paused for a picnic on a wooden bench that had been carved with a very Mindful inscription.

"If a blade of grass springing up in the fields has power to move you, rejoice, for your soul is alive". Eleonora Duse (1858 - 1924).

I discovered that this lady was an Italian actress contemporaneous with the great Sarah Bernhardt.

The changes that we see throughout our lives are varied yet many things such as our wonder of the natural world remains a constant thread to hold on to whatever the weather.

Episode 3 - Baskets of Plenty

Psalm 16 : 2, 11
I say to the Lord, "you are my Lord;
all the good things I have come from you".
You will show me the path that leads to life;
your presence fills me with joy and
brings me pleasure forever.

The title of this Episode in fact refers to spiritual gifts or blessings as much as to food, drink, rich robes or other bounty. We have so much to be grateful for although it's not always that easy to say. At the time of writing the news is full of hardship, the cost of living crisis, the rising price of energy and the huge difficulties even working people are facing just to put food on the table. It's been a very tough three years as we emerge as a nation from a dreadful pandemic and prices for groceries have soared. Today I am giving thanks that there is food in my pantry and I didn't have to rely on a Food Parcel for four months. That is a huge celebration as everyone wants a measure of independence and I enjoy the freedom of being able to buy food. But people are really struggling and the only thing I can advise is to lower your sights.

Thankfulness is power, rejoice in what you have and tuck your regrets away onto the back burner to deal with when you can put them right. Looking ahead, later in this book I look at the pros and cons of making a retrograde step as sometimes it's appropriate to consider if going back is a way forward. Also at the time of writing our allies in Ukraine have been invaded by Russia and all we hear is how this is to blame for the rising cost of energy. It's nothing new so I found a poem by the Victorian novelist

Thomas Hardy (1840 - 1928) where he looked up from his writing to see the full moon beaming down. When the author asked the moon what he was so interested in, the moon explained that he was looking for a man in the lake. The man had become overborn with grief at losing his son in a senseless war. In contrast to this dark message, in Hardy's poem "The Darkling Thrush" the poet writes of the bird singing cheerfully as if it had "some blessed hope, whereof he knew And I was unaware".

Hope, the only human quality left in Pandora's box, keeps a perspective but is more easy in a warm, comfortable home with food in one's tummy than out in the driving rain, wind and snow. In the opera "Turandot" by Giacomo Puccini the ice cold Princess sets three riddles for any aspirant to her hand in marriage and if he fails the penalty is death. Many men die in the attempt but an unknown Prince from afar guesses all three correctly. The third riddle is " what dies in the night and is reborn every morning?" The answer is hope but the unknown Prince wants Turandot to love him so he gives her a second chance asking her to guess his name before dawn. Finally he sings "nessun dorma" which means none shall sleep then in the morning he reveals his name - Calaf. Princess Turandot falls into his arms and peace is restored to the land.

In another opera by Puccini, "Tosca", the heroine is a beautiful opera singer in love with a political activist. Scarpia, the evil Chief of Police, desires her and plans the arrest and execution of Cavaradossi, her lover. Scarpia offers to save the activist's life if Tosca will submit to him. Tosca plunges a dagger, thus murdering Scarpia but then when Cavaradossi is shot by a firing squad, Tosca plunges over the parapet of the Castle meeting her own death below. No happy ending here but some utterly sumptuous music including Tosca's aria "visi d'arte, visi d'amore" where she sings, "I have lived for art, I have lived for music. Why has fate rewarded me thus?"

It reminds me of our Bath buskers or street musicians doing Puccini badly but I assure you if you hear it done properly by trained singers it is divine.

II.

UPSKILL IN A DOWNTURN

Episode 1 - Sorrow and Loss

Psalm 65: 1-3
O God, it is right for us to praise you in Zion
and keep our promises to you,
because you answer prayers.
People everywhere will come to you
on account of their sins.
Our faults defeat us, but you forgive them.

As a child, I was often the despair of my mother as I loved to walk through the fields to and from school getting my smart shoes covered in mud in the meantime. School was difficult so this metime in the countryside gave me complete mindfulness and escapism as I became observant of the changing of the seasons while learning to be very quiet and careful as I walked past the bull or the ram. I loved solitary rambles at the weekend too, walking up the mountain stream in plimsolls to admire the rock formations and cascading waterfalls. This is still to me my most enthusiastic form of worship, in the great outdoors with birdsong and frog spawn. Perhaps that would be a simple explanation as to how I failed to thrive in big cities because even the bigger parks would seem overly artificial. It is to my mother in particular that I owe this love of Nature as she taught me all the names of wild flowers. In those days they would bloom in an ordered sequence; catkins first then celandines followed by violets with bluebells appearing as late as May. Nowadays they all seem to come at once and the bluebells are much earlier, appearing as soon as March if it's mild.

My mother lost her own mother at quite a young age, there was a little baby boy that would have been my uncle but he died of pneumonia and my maternal grandmother followed soon after. So all things considered my mother was a survivor who did the best job she could while enduring much hardship and penury. She even travelled to Bath to look after me when I had my wisdom teeth out, bringing a big bunch of flowers and cooking me her childhood speciality, soft boiled egg with bread and butter in a cup mixed together. She also went with me to Tenby on the train as my depression was starting to appear. She was very accepting, broad minded, never self flagellated, and was always really supportive.

In 1991 amidst training in the laboratory while having a go at my driving test, I took a walking holiday to the Pindos Mountains in Northern Greece which are close to the border with Albania. Such a glorious two weeks of getting away from it all with two guides and a van to carry our luggage. It was a group of quite mixed characters from different walks of life with a common goal to enjoy the peace of these stunning mountains. We started our walk in a magnificent gorge cutting through the rocks with cold springs that we bathed in followed by a siesta in the shade. During that fortnight we climbed Mount Smolikos which is Greece's second highest peak after Mount Olympus. We camped under the stars, sang around the campfire and looked out for the prints of bear paws in the woods. We finished the walk in a Greek town called Ioannina which was famous for its silver filigree jewellery and from there we travelled by ferry back to the airport on the Island of Corfu. Once back in Bath I finally managed to pass my driving test on the fourth attempt reminding me of my school violin teacher. She said that if one is good at sport then you would be good at playing the violin because it requires coordination, no hope there then so I wasn't very coordinated on the pitch, in the music room or in the car. Perhaps writing has been my strong point for much longer and being academic just came more naturally.

Episode 2 - To Smile Again

Psalm 33: 1-3
All you that are righteous, shout for joy for what
the Lord has done; praise him, all you that obey him.
Give thanks to the Lord with harps,
sing to him with stringed instruments.
Sing a new song to him, play the harp with skill,
and shout for joy!

The facing page shows a slightly darker, winter scene of the bandstand in Hedgemead Park Bath where we enjoyed a couple of hours taking photographs and generally observing the trees, landscape and surrounding architecture. It was February and the periwinkle was in flower while the bandstand was silent and empty before bursting into life by spring bank holiday. I am reminded of my childhood as my mother and I would walk from our home to Ynysyngharad Park in Pontypridd for the brass band concerts on a Sunday afternoon during the summer holidays. My favourite was "Lily the Pink", and there are words as follows:-

> "We'll drink a drink a drink to Lily the Pink,
> the Pink, the Pink,
> The saviour of the human race,
> For she invented medicinal compound,
> Most applicatious in every case!"

There is more but I will stop there!

I discovered that taking photographs is really mindful, all other considerations melt away as I look for suitable subjects then work really hard to get them suitably focussed and composed well to make them interesting. It was such a therapeutic past time where all my worries and cares would be completely forgotten for a few hours then if I had them printed they would be hung up on my wall as a lasting memento of that perfectly peaceful time. I am also amazed at how a full brass band complete with instruments and music stands can all fit into that tiny bandstand space. It's moments like these that make every minute count, the here and now is our only reality as sometimes looking backwards makes me flinch and looking forwards is just a great unknown.

Episode 3 - Defying Nature

William Wordsworth (1770 - 1850)
from Upon Westminster Bridge
September 3rd. 1802
Dull would he be of soul who could pass by
A sight so touching in its majesty:

I remember meeting a person who took several hundred photographs of the outside of a famous cathedral but didn't go inside. Well it's true that visiting any place of interest can be an expensive hobby but I was intrigued. Was it because of the darkness of the interior which is not good for picture taking? Was it the smell of incense and candle wax that put them off? Did this person have enough time to go inside but just preferred the exterior of the iconic building? I will never know. William Wordsworth wrote the above poem for the Palace of Westminster and the Abbey there but notice that he wrote from the bridge that is of course on the outside.The first line of this poem is "Earth has not anything to show more fair". The architecture is of course human made so we could argue all day and night that a natural landscape is far more lovely than anything created by mere mortals. We can consider this question whatever our beliefs are, whether we think that the world was created in seven days by the Almighty or took millions of aeons of time and evolution. There is no doubt that architecture is pleasing to the eye but even though I live in a pretty city I know where I stand and to quote another song,"I'd rather be a forest than a street". I love to see the woods carpeted with wild garlic in April. There is no greater pleasure than spotting the wild pasque flower in our city's botanical gardens where there is a wild area that seems even nicer than the cultivated borders of forced begonias. But to live we must build shelter, burn energy and grow food for the masses all of which takes its toll on the landscape. Is anywhere truly unspoilt? I remember when I was in America a good friend from the church said that she would take me hiking. So we drove to the walking area and then walked amongst the 'live' trees that are evergreen but it was a ramblers park with a trail then afterwards we drove to the restaurant before going home. My favourite experience out there was Canyon Lake which has a dam. I have painted this scene from memory and the complete serenity of that place really was very beautiful. It came back to me as I painted which was a very enjoyable thing to do even though my artistic skill is no big deal but once finished the water colour takes me straight back. I was there at first light after looking it up on the map - no sat nav in those days! As I am writing today it is March, we've had snow that has just turned to heavy rain and it's a far cry from Texas where we climbed Enchanted Rock in T-shirts in January. I really believe that the opportunity to travel was one thing I valued most about my time in science as well as the International community described further on.

III.
THIS JOYFUL LIFE

Episode 1 - Use Time Productively

Dylan Thomas (1914 - 1953) from Fern Hill
Oh as I was young and easy in the mercy of his means,
Time held me green and dying
Though I sang in my chains like the sea.

I utterly love this last line from the poem by Dylan Thomas, thinking of the sea and how its gentle, lapping murmur can change in an instance to an overpowering roar that needs to be respected at all times. I remember spending spring and summer holidays at Weymouth on the Jurassic Coast when I would travel by double decker bus to Lyme Regis. There I loved the seaside gardens and would enjoy the effect of the ammonite decorations on the lamp posts with a stunning view of the bay. One time I was there I watched a wind surfer who was riding the waves into the shore then going back out to sea to ride into land again and again. The wind surfer was very skilled but after a lot of wave rolling they began to fall off more often as if getting exhausted. The sun was shining and I also visited Lyme Regis museum to see real ammonites and a great ichthyosaurus which was the first recorded sighting of a dinosaur fossil in the Victorian era. This fossil resembles a large turtle but with a beak suggesting the pterodactyls that are thought to be ancestors of our modern birds. It has a pointed end and puts me in mind of the pelican's beak.

The sea played a significant role in the Industrial Revolution when huge cargos of coal and pig iron would be transported by ship out of Cardiff Docks. I remember seeing Cardiff Bay before it had its makeover, the barrage was only a suggestion when I was in College, the River Taff was tidal and when the tide was out, there were mud flats exposed, littered with old, discarded supermarket trolleys and other detritus. In the Bible, I think it's the Old Testament, it says "do not ask why was it so much better in the old days? It's not an intelligent question." Yet looking back is a very human failing, when I was only seventeen we used to say that children's television isn't what it was. Well, as I write amidst a storm of rain, the sun is trying to come through the clouds and so far we've had no more snow. I am glad really, if I can save on the heating bills at this difficult time then I am grateful for small mercies.

Episode 2 - Consider the Universe

Psalm 139: 1-3
Lord, you have examined me and you know me.
You know everything I do; from far away you
understand all my thoughts.
You see me, whether I am working or resting;
you know all my actions.

Psalm 139 speaks, or should I say sings, of the total completeness of God's knowledge of the people he created. It describes this knowledge as loving no matter where we are, whether we are busy or at leisure, and he knows our needs before we express them. This acknowledgement on our part means that all our aspirations are recognized by God who has the wisdom to say " yes, no or wait" as he knows what is really in our best interests. Yesterday, when the snow that was forecast didn't fall but was replaced by rain then a thaw, I wrote a poem for my muse. Here it is with its often repeated pledge that no writer's life is complete without an object to write for and a reader to enjoy the finished product.

SWEET MUSE

Drops of rain come streaming down
Late blossoms are delayed
Rejoicing in my love for you
I remember younger days

When we were strong
No threat too large
Was tackled, fought and killed

A problem shared, defeated not
For we took on our world

My love for you will never die
Esteem is vibrant still
For underneath that baseball cap
Lurk brains and iron will

Ron we love you to the end
I'll go where you go too
For when your earthly race is run
My life belongs to you.

In fact our contact is very limited these days but at one time I would speak to him on the phone quite regularly. The physicality just didn't occur, I have seven muse and number three said "Meryl, a shag is a sea bird". I replied "yes, for some of us it is". So today is a Sunday and off the top of my head I will write another poem for my most recently acquired muse, the estimable reverend seven.

TO MY STETHOSCOPE

Work, work, work, no sleep, no rest
It's booming in my head
Your heart beat is my daily grind
This tiny life is saved

For every grain of sand at sea
Is counted by our God
Our hair, our cells, our very skin
So precious all of us to Him
We pledge to act where're we can
Refer this baby for a scan

But I am older, still I count
Now you are there for me
Another's hand wields instruments
Ah yes, ah yes, I see!

My time will one day run its race
Then sickness is no more
But while I live in service thus
I'll pray, I'll stay, I'll talk

The Gospel is my rock and stay
Your comfort my endeavour
When you're in need, I'm there at speed
For now and then forever.

Here is a photo I took of a neighbourhood cat poised to pounce on some creature in the undergrowth of the woodlands. The cat is very mindful, not focussing on any issue other than the catch of something good to eat. Then perhaps it is also faced with landing on its feet from a higher perch which must involve concentration. The cat didn't even appear to notice me taking its photo, it seemed oblivious of the distraction of the click of my phone. What an important way to be, but as humans there are so many distractions. I feel completely focussed as I write, my thoughts are not wandering except to think of the reader eventually making the most of this perusal and perhaps enjoying the colour pictures. If you like the book send me a post of feedback on Facebook.

Episode 3 - Reflecting Back

William Butler Yeats (1865 - 1939)
from The Lake Isle of Innisfree
I will arise and go now, for always night and day
I hear lake water lapping with low sounds by the shore;
While I stand on the roadway, or on the pavements grey,
I hear it in the deep heart's core.

I spent eight months living and working in San Antonio, Texas between September 1992 and April 1993. Staff at the Health Science Center came from all corners of the globe and once a month we would meet on a Friday evening for the International Alliance. These were gatherings where there would be a presentation on a different country with an accompanying buffet. Here I made friends from England, Finland and Australia. With two of these friends I visited Natural Bridge Caverns and Natural Bridge Wildlife Ranch, so called because of a bridge in the rock that had been worn and eroded underneath by time to cause a beautiful arch across the entrance to the caves.

The caverns were filled with glorious, underground stalagmites and stalactites in a magnificent display like a natural cathedral. We were asked not to touch any of the calcified stone so as not to cause any erosion or chemical change with the enzymes on our fingers. When we reached the end of our tour, there was an upright, calcified stalagmite next to the trail that we were allowed to touch. With all the passing of many, many visitors this stone had worn black and smooth.

At the Wildlife Ranch, we bought bird food which the ostriches loved. The eager bird reached its long neck into the car to put its beak into the carton of food. I had to put the feed outside the car then once the ostrich moved with the food we closed the window up quickly and slowly went on through the Ranch. We also saw buffalo which are becoming very rare. I was relocated back to England in that spring and my kind colleagues gave me a sumptuous leaving do, in my favourite restaurant with a magnificent birthday cake to follow. I received a gift of a mug with the Health Science Centre coat of arms on it, also a notebook and pen. I had to hand in all my white coats then fly to Houston before boarding the plane to Gatwick, London. I stayed for six months with a relative in Wales then returned to Bath. While I was living in Abergavenny I walked to the top of Holy Mountain where there was once rumoured to be a monastery destroyed by a landslide. The local legend has it that the Devil put his foot down and in fact if you travel by road or train past the hillside you can see where the land looks as though it has fallen down in a slip. The views from the top are stunning, across the seven hills of Abergavenny and beyond with the Brecon Beacons to the West, Hay on Wye further East then Herefordshire further up. Hay on Wye is famous for its many second hand bookshops where I went to find some out of print titles that my father collected in his lifetime. Hereford has a beautiful, rose pink cathedral with original Norman Arches along the Nave and Perpendicular Arches in the side aisles that were added later.

In 2015 there were big celebrations for the 800th anniversary of Magna Carta, that famous bill of rights the English barons imposed upon King John in 1215. There are four surviving copies of this ancient manuscript, written in Latin, on sheepskin using quill pens and ink made from wasps gall. Amongst the celebrations an exhibition was held in Hereford Cathedral of some beautiful banners depicting the calligraphy or ancient script. This just held my attention so much, the banners hung down from between the rose sandstone columns of this amazing building. I could never fathom out why I should love Hereford more than any other cathedral or abbey. There is just something about the magic of its waterside location that leaves a lasting memory even defying me to attempt to photograph it. It houses the mapa mundi and a very famous chained library, also the last time I was there they were still using an old boiler from the beginning of the 20th Century. Everything about that visit was fantastic, even the bronze bull in the Market Square, a symbol of the county's commerce. I found a similar bronze bull in Oxford the last time I was there. It never ceases to amaze me that a sculptor can work such a miracle as to cast an animal or human in bronze, marble or wood. Back to my city of domicile which is Bath, there are lovely botanical gardens and a dead tree has been carved into a Totem Pole which I pause to admire thinking to myself "how do they do that and where do they start?"

Sometimes readers say to me "where do you get your ideas from?" I think it pays to be mindful and observant, if we only take the trouble to raise our eyes from our own, sometimes obsessive cares and concerns we could feel completely different as we take in the beauties of the world around us. Then we might feel less fixated with all the misery and negativity of the news.

IV.
DIVERGENT PATHS

Episode 1 - Awareness is Born

Robert Frost (1874 - 1963)
From Stopping By Woods on a Snowy Evening.
The woods are lovely, dark and deep,
But I have promises to keep,
And miles to go before I sleep,
And miles to go before I sleep.

EQUESTRIAN JOY

Fluid in motion, strong, bold lines
The horses coats shine
With plaited manes
As plumes aloft
Decorations fit for a king

Side step, trot, now forward go
Jumping over barricades so
Prize winning at every show
Four legs in perfect harmony
A pat to encourage, a word in your ear
Horse and rider now as one
With the whole joyful company

Dancing, prancing, all in step
While soldiers salute
The monarch, his consort
A gathered entranced audience

Clapping in wondered awe
A tradition every year
Ever new forever more.

UPHOLDING THE LAW

Belshazzar, a king from long ago
Drank wine from vessels golden, pure
Taken from the holy Temple fair

As guests drank down insensate so
A hand appeared with writing lo
But none it's word could read

The writing on the wall was seen
As the king grew pale with fear
So Daniel came, the prophet spoke
Of kings and sins before

You are found light upon the scales
Young Daniel did declare
That night Belshazzar met his end
But a new king came to rule

While Daniel prayed at window side
His enemies planned his end
And to the lions he was thrown
But angels God did send

Now Daniel saved, restored to life
Detractors were no more
His proven innocence saved his life
Under a golden rule.

Go out about your business thus
While bearing this in mind
The scales are balanced
Tilted thus as good all evil defied.

BANQUETS OF BLISS

Feasting from an online shop
A full larder, blessings galore
Casting my mind to manna
As the taste from heaven came

Gathered around, the angels sang
To welcome sinners home
Come feast with us forever more
A repast that's ours alone

While heads of state robe up to greet
A host from all the world
Forget not how the Lord provides
What's his that comes to his own

So many starve, so many die
For want of basic need
Give thanks unto the God above
For bounty bought online

Delivered directly to my door
Such joy to last a month
No waste, no bags, all new to me
Can't wait to start again.

DEFENDING THE FAITH

Like an ant hill, with roles to play
A hierarchy takes control today
While workers toil to feed the nation
A humble scribbler has this to say:-

I'm fairly low upon the ladder
My baseline broad and strong
Considering our lot in life
A triangle to the sky

The bottom line our feet of clay
Our Council half way up
Atop with orb and sceptre held
His Majesty before his deity
Ultimately filled with responsibility
Positioned with good things to say

His Christmas message fills with hope
The joy of all concerned
A thank you for us, everyone
More grit, determination won
As tough times call for all of us
To pull as yesteryear

Many faiths inhabit England
Our church is just a part
But while we are alive today
Give thanks with a grateful heart.

OUR TINY OFFERING

I'm sending you a present
It's not for you to eat
This tiny little mustard seed
For your garden quite complete

You plant it in the springtime
The Lord will send the rain
Then year on year you'll be amazed
At its girth, it's leaves, it's frame

If you have a penny
Each time you spend it so
By a year it's grown into
A faith of an apostle as if
The Lord had willed it grow

With faith we'll win in triumph
Our harvest won't be slow
One tiny, precious mustard seed
A tree as it is now.

FOR KING CHARLES III

Any one or all of us
Have sometime lost our Mum
But taking up the reigns of State
Takes strength to carry on

We expect miracles of our leaders
They're just a human too
So let's applaud His Majesty
For his dignity and aplomb

He waited in the wings
With patient tenacity
So now at last
He's crowned our King
With pomp and ceremony
Watched by millions
Nerves of steel, after
His first Christmas message
That brought such harmony

He thanked the humble Food Bank
The army on the ground
Each volunteer heard praise indeed
In personal greeting warm and sound

So here's to new beginnings
A gardener at the helm
Sustainable for all time
Rejoice for now then moving on
We serve, we grow, we thrive.

I started writing poetry at the age of forty one in 2007 when I had spent many years in a range of voluntary roles. I have served in a charity shop, helped with an art and craft group and organised a peer support group for mental health. The work was rewarding but I love to write so in this section I have included my most recent poetry written in March 2023 to provide something cheerful when the news continues to be grim.

Episode 2 - This Mindful Experience

Christina Rossetti (1830 - 1894)
From Remember.
Yet if you should forget me for a while
And afterwards remember, do not grieve:
For if the darkness and corruption leave
A vestige of the thoughts that once I had,
Better by far you should forget and smile
Than that you should remember and be sad.

The image opposite shows a rug I made out of crocheted yarn. For those who have yet to try this technique, I will briefly explain that crochet is attempted with a single hook rather than the two needles that are used in knitting. Because this rug was intended for the floor, rather than over one's knees, I have chosen a dense, close pattern that you will see has no holes or lacy design. The colours were a somewhat random mix of blues and greens with the whole finished off with a black, shell pattern border.

I find that the activity of crochet is a really good distraction that absorbs me in a mindful way without any intrusive thought patterns or dwelling on outside issues. I find I have to concentrate quite hard to get it right and the big advantage of crochet for me is that there is only one stitch so it's easy to put it right if I go wrong. The slightly tedious part of the job is the putting together of all the squares while sewing in all the loose ends of all the different colours where they have been added. This can be done with a darning needle but here I used a finer crochet hook to give the rustic effect of the seams. It's a cold weather task that keeps me focused and was ideal for the Covid 19 pandemic when going out was very much restricted. You could also call it a 'resting writer's job'.

As I write today I am enjoying the sight of two bunches of carnations that have the scent of cloves. There are white flowers and the other vase is filled with yellow carnations tipped with red. My geraniums are flowering on the window sill and I am attempting to grow cauliflower from seeds. I have been to the garden to change the water in my bird bath, noticing as I do that the birds have eaten all the mealworms, all the bug pellets and most of the seeds I put out just a few days ago. They must be feeding their young as the food didn't disappear that quickly before. Mindful activities such as these keep me sane and helped during the monotony of three lock downs.

Episode 3 - The Unique Challenge

Stevie Smith 1903 - 1971
From Not Waving But Drowning.
I was much further out than you thought
And not waving but drowning.

So what was or is the unique challenge? Well, I had awful mental health issues throughout my adult life and had to reinvent myself on coming home from Texas USA. But they say it's very common, yes regrettably I have attended far too many funerals of people I knew through the day centre and experienced plenty of stigma. The greatest stigma must have been because I have no children and have devoted the last fifteen years of my life to my literature while all the jobs I applied for did not result in a single interview. Perhaps it's now my age, they were asking me could I be an age friendly employer? Trouble is, I do all my writing, research and photography myself so I would struggle to give an employee enough to do. Sometimes I think people are just struggling to find a topic of conversation on the bus, have a go at me because of the way they're feeling or are lacking in their own self esteem. Who was it, said, "no-one can make you feel small without your consent"?

V.

FULL CIRCLE

Episode 1 - Chasing One's Tail

Romans 8: 31
In view of all this, what can we say?
If God is for us, who can be against us?

I attended a service in Bath Abbey for Pentecost one Sunday in, I think, 2009 and we heard of the people gathered listening to the Good News in their own languages. I know very little Welsh but the following day I took a train to Cardiff then a bus to Pontypridd after a gap of almost twenty years. I visited Ynysyngharad Park where a new War memorial had been built, again like the park itself it was put up by public subscription. I have not been back since, I was told that I'd find big changes but to me it all looked the same except that the shopping precinct had been bulldozed. I spent thirteen years living near Ponty but left at eighteen for College in Cardiff, before that we lived at Beddau pronounced bather. It's a long time ago and this weekend has seen the Coronation of King Charles III and Queen Consort Camilla so it's now a very different world. There were women bishops and choristers at the service which I followed on the Radio, that had never been seen at an English coronation before.

Episode 2 - Retrograde or Not?

John 20: 29
*Jesus said to him, "Do you believe because you see me?
How happy are those who believe without seeing me!"*

In my first Novella, "The Judge Jones Trilogy", the two barristers discuss their heavy caseload in a fictitious roof top garden set at the top of the City Court House. The scene is inspired by the elegant roof garden in Cardiff Castle where I enjoyed an utterly amazing guided tour. There are one hundred and eighty steps to the clock tower but it was worth it and if you also manage to climb to the top of the keep there are panoramic views of the city with the faux mediaeval folly of Castle Coch to the north. Coch is Welsh for red and the Ch is pronounced as in Bach the composer so it's Castle Corch not Cock as one ghastly TV presenter put it.

The surroundings of Cardiff Castle are equally magnificent with forty acres of Parkland on the bank of the River Taff. There is now a jetty where one can step aboard a power dinghy bound for Cardiff Bay where a freshwater lake has been created out of River water. It's possible to see cormorants holding out their wings to dry and there are pleasure cruises in season.

I left school at Pontypridd in 1984 then decided on the advice of a friend's Mum to apply to Llandaff College in Cardiff to read Applied Life Sciences. For A levels, my best result was in Biology and this had interested me the most. I was very privileged to be given a place at the interview and I also visited a working medical laboratory in my local hospital. The direction of the course was to train diagnosticians who are the people behind the scenes, receiving your sample when you give one at the surgery. On my course leading to B.Sc., we had practical training in addition to lectures on the theory behind many human disorders.

Some people think that my expertise was gained in the United States of America but no my early training gave me more knowledge and a broad education. My PhD doctorate was studied in Bath, then after all that I crossed the pond to Texas on an academic exchange with a visitor's visa. So once I graduated from Cardiff I was employed to undertake research in London, Bath then USA and paid income tax on both sides of the Atlantic.

For BSc the final year included research training for an honours dissertation and I was very privileged to work at the Cancer Centre at Velindre in Cardiff for three months and was also permitted to work on the subject of my own choosing after reading current literature. For this I am hugely indebted to my tutor and the team at the research laboratories. At Velindre I had a lot of autonomy which was never repeated. Once I gained a foothold in medical research there were many senior scientists who said to me " your results do not agree with my prediction so you must have made a mistake". In response I would search for literature that agreed with my findings but it was all very much a disillusionment after my positive time in Cardiff.
My College tutor and I did have one important thing in common, neither of us likes being made use of. We will put our shoulders to the wheel, pull an emotional muscle to help then grumble afterwards. My one wish is that he writes his own autobiography so that he can get mad safely with the people who he felt were holding him back as he left teaching for a consultancy role. Academics are just people in an ivory tower (who knows what we mean by that?) and

possibly it was just one person grumbling and it felt as if everyone was doing that.

I asked him for a lift once for the sake of quality time in the car, at that early stage my depression was starting to show and I needed the support. I never lived it down but the last time we spoke he had concerns that didn't bother me. Maybe I wasn't very empathic, I'm so sorry and just want to say that my life is hardly enhanced one bit now for having a PhD but my life is totally enriched for having met you. My own beautiful mother once said that I did better by choosing a "red brick university" rather than a more snobby one. I received first class training, my Alma mater made it all possible and I feel all the gratitude one would wish.

I found time in London for theatre, ballet, opera and classical concerts because I was earning. It's all less important to me now, I had hundreds of concert programmes with the finest performers so I donated them to charity. Youth is wasted on the young they say and you can never quite recapture that first fine careless rapture. No I don't want to go backwards just forwards out of here as a nurse once put it.

Episode 3 - Resilience and Strength

Dylan Thomas (1914 - 1953)
From Do Not Go Gentle Into That Good Night
Old age should burn and rave at close of day;
Rage, rage against the dying of the light.

The photograph shows a scene from the Hedgemead Park in Bath with the spire of St Swithin's church, Walcot Street. It's said to be the church where William Wilberforce (1759 - 1833) married and when my father was alive we visited the Museum dedicated to the late MP in Hull, Yorkshire. Wilberforce had been a rigorous campaigner in Parliament in the quest to abolish slavery. The museum showed what conditions were like aboard a slave trade vessel with the appalling cramped conditions with all their ensuing sickness and disease. Wilberforce was an MP for 50 years and died just before his abolition bill was passed. My father must have known this visit to the museum was just what interests me and perhaps without me realising, I picked up my interest in social policy from a family that always enjoys commenting on current affairs.

My late mother was inclined to buy a quality newspaper every day but her other interest was ornithology or the study of birds. When I came home from Texas I was free to take her out and about as I had a little car. We went with one of my sisters to the National Garden Show in Ebbw Vale at a time when these schemes to develop green space were opening up across the country. Then I took my mother to see a falconry display in Barry, South Wales which was amazing. They have these big birds of prey that fly to the handler from a perch then the bird receives a reward of food. I think my mother and I really enjoyed this and afterwards we went to the beach where Mam paddled in the sea with me.

I'm the youngest of six children so my mother was forty years old when I was born. She had served in the Women's Air Force for nine months during World War II alongside my aunty who was my mother's twin. My mother said only a little about that time, she said it was the only time she put on any weight as she was decently fed, and she reminisced about the men she met. An Irishman who was exceptionally homesick and another man who played the banjo. My father tells me that he'd met her on a bus while she said that she came to Wales to contact someone else then changed her mind and met my Dad. He says they did their courting sometimes in the swimming pool so once I was grown up I took her to Swansea Leisure centre where there was a wave machine. She did enjoy that although by then she was pretty much over father. She never remarried but he did and moved to Yorkshire, hence the visit to Hull and a boat trip across Scarborough Bay - thank you to you both. John Dryden (1631 - 1700) was the first English Poet Laureate and said "tomorrow do thy worst for I have lived today". Amen to that.

VI.

END OF THE TUNNEL

Episode 1 - The New Dawn

1 Peter 1: 3
*Let us give thanks to the God and Father of our
Lord Jesus Christ! Because of his great mercy he gave
us new life by raising Jesus Christ from death.
This fills us with a living hope.*

The stories from the New Testament of the Bible have inspired many numbers of artists and paintings, sculptures or literature. When I sang in my College choir we performed in a festival of nine lessons and carols in Llandaff Cathedral every year at Christmas. The choir stalls or seats are just underneath the magnificent soaring arch that supports Epstein's Majestus, an aluminium statue of the ascending Lord Jesus Christ, and this arch with its concrete pillar also houses the organ pipes. The statue of Jesus in a seamless robe is cast without wounds, something I also noticed about the painting Christ of St John of the Cross by Salvador Dali, that I saw in Glasgow. This shows the crucified Lord above the Sea of Galilee with the fishermen and their boat. It originally hung in the Kelvingrove Art Gallery where you could admire the painting at the end of a long corridor so you could stand well back and view it from more distance. It needed the space to do it justice. I bought a reproduction for a friend and she still has it in her lounge even though for my own part I said that I wouldn't give it houseroom.

Episode 2 - Emerging Chrysalis

1 John 3: 2-3
My dear friends, we are now God's children, but it is not yet clear what we shall become. But we know that when Christ appears, we shall be like him, because we shall see him as he really is. Everyone who has this hope in Christ keeps himself pure, just as Christ is pure.

Perhaps the painting and sculpture mentioned in VI 1 above were inspired by this part of the Bible where Christ's wounds are healed. Revelations Chapter 21 describes "a new heaven and a new earth" and "He will wipe away every tear".

AFTER THE END

All tears have now been shed,
I lay my grief to rest
My burden cast aside
The Lord has turned the tide.

I'm going to a party
My God has penned a list,
For every guest is welcome
When all has seemed amiss.

The pain of angst and crying
Will never more be seen,
The gates of all new Zion
Are ours to walk right in.

Our Holy, sacred city
Is not for us to sack
There is no greater judgement
Arising from our lack.

So at the end of all time
We may find food enough
The manna or the nectar
All goodness from above.

Episode 3 - Don't look back

Gerard Manley Hopkins (1844-89)
From God's Grandeur
And for all this, nature is never spent;
There lives the dearest freshness deep down things;

Christoph Wilibaud Gluck was an opera composer in the 18th century and in his opera "Orpheus and Eurydice" the drama tells the story of the triumph of love over even death itself. Eurydice, the bride of Orpheus, dies after a snake bite then descends to Hades (hell). Her husband is inconsolable and pleads with Amore the god of love to allow him to go to find her. Jove takes pity but Amore sets the condition that Orpheus must not look at his wife nor explain why he mustn't do so.

Orpheus sings soulfully at the gates of hell and finds his bride in the Elysian Fields but she doesn't understand his apparent indifference as he turns his face from her to lead her away back to life. Eurydice sings that life without her husband means nothing and she dies once more. Orpheus forgets his vow and turns to hold her in his arms then wants to take his own life. Amore the god of love prevents this and finally is moved to pity, then Eurydice is restored to life. All the assembled throng sing praises to love and all ends happily.

It's a classical legend but very allegorical; there are many pleading voices in my life asking "why don't you go back into science?" Or worse still "have you ever thought about going back to Wales?" Perhaps I am somewhat sensitive but I find both these suggestions extremely irritating, no one can go backwards and to suggest that my present needs me to change that much is something I find quite frankly to be discriminatory. I discovered one Sunday that 'busy body' is a word in the Bible although I couldn't quote Chapter and Verse.

I wrote above about my College years which were very happy, so now I will remember just a little of my earlier career in school. I was academic and totally rubbish at sport but I found the most fantastic experience spending my lunch breaks and weekends out with others doing the Bronze, Silver and Gold Duke of Edinburgh Award. Thanks here are due to kind, hardworking teachers who put in extra time to support us with the various hobbies, hiking and service interests that had to be covered to attain the awards. For bronze I did cookery and learnt to swim a length, for silver I read the novels of Jane Austen and for Gold we raised money for charity, did aerobics and studied a famous French person. The hike was in the Brecon Beacons (Bannau Breciniog), it snowed and it was a once in a lifetime experience. Four of us went to St James Palace to receive the certificate which I still have and a badge. My friend's brother wore his naval cubs uniform so the Duke of Edinburgh spoke with him then addressed the group with good humour. Us ladies had to wear a hat which my mother never forgot as she also wore the most dear, little straw for my PhD graduation.

All the other aspects of school life I would like to conveniently forget, I remember vividly receiving far more respect from the staff when I entered the sixth form. I became a senior prefect then when voted for by my peers, I hadn't been a prefect the year before when the staff did the choosing. I have heard people say "we treat them all the same" but when will authority learn that everyone is an individual? Everyone is unique and everyone has a story that is entitled to be heard. Some people have enormous egos but miniscule self esteem. To respect yourself, start with gratitude and respect to those who gave so much that we might live and grow in our own esteem. Getting back to my College tutor, he said "Meryl is small in stature but great in character", what an unforgettable accolade now put in my short story Jimmy's Garden. With faith in me like that, how can I lose?

VII.

SELF-RELIANCE FOR NEWBIES

Episode 1 - Tell Out My Soul

Acts 4: 20
*For we cannot stop speaking of what
we ourselves have seen and heard.*

In 2005, at the end of August, I visited the City of Dublin to see the book of Kells. This is an ancient, Medieval manuscript written by the monks of old. They wrote using goose or swan feathers, using ink made from wasps gall and illuminated the documents with pigments in bright colours that have survived even to this day. The book of Kells, containing the four gospels, is on display at Trinity College Dublin which was founded by Queen Elizabeth I in an attempt to provide a Protestant seat of learning that she hoped would settle unrest. I understand that the curators of this very precious book turn a page every so often to show more of the manuscript to visitors if they go twice.

I flew to Dublin then caught a bus into the city centre where I stayed in a good Bed and Breakfast that was within reasonable walking distance of the sights. There is a lot to see; I visited Christchurch Cathedral to see Strongbow's tomb dating back to the Normans. Strongbow was a knight who had conquered, at a battle in Ireland, and married the daughter of the Duke of Leinster. In the National Portrait Gallery of Ireland there is a huge, wall sized painting of this wedding with the firebrand priest surrounded by an array of bodies from the battle.

One thing that is very popular with tourists is the open top bus, in Dublin it drives past the house where the Taesoch lives and the guide pointed out the candle that is lit in the window at all times to welcome returning Irish home. Taesoch means teacher and this position is the leader of parliament which in 2005 was a woman. During my stay in Dublin I also took a bus to Powers court gardens which are at the foot of the Wicklow mountains, in the shadow of a hill called The Sugar Loaf because of its shape. There is a sugar loaf mountain in Abergavenny also and is there not one in South Africa?

I visited St Stephen's shopping centre on my last day and nearby there is a garden with a statue of Oscar Wilde. The whole holiday lasted seven days and I packed a lot in, including a visit to St James Gate for the old brewery, at the very top of the building is the Gravity Bar with 360 degree views looking out over the whole of Dublin. It's bigger than I realised, bigger than Cardiff at any rate.

Episode 2 - Finding Peace

Alfred Lord Tennyson (1809 - 1892) from Ulysses
For always roaming with a hungry heart
Much have I seen and known.

From the Bible, I once heard a lady vicar speak these words, "do not take away the dream of the poor". Then, many years ago, someone I met said "if you can just achieve a stage in your journey towards your dream then you will feel better in yourself even if you don't make all the dream". I had dreams that were mostly about myself, I wanted a doctorate, I wanted to live and work in America then I wanted to come home. Once all of that proved doable I settled back in Bath and began to write but sometimes I wrote to others' suggestions and it was no longer all about me. It was my late father who was keen for me to get published so it has happened even though he didn't live to see it. Nowadays I am very conscious of the fact that many people have been kind enough to give feedback, to acquire my work and to collect new books in a way that is massively rewarding. One of my sisters found it hard to understand how I managed working in the laboratory when all of it was done solo, the writing up was all done solo then finally the supervisor and examiners stepped in and then one's contract is over but it's on with the motley. Looking back it does seem a bit unreal, a lovely person I met also found it hard to grasp that my work involved bottles and tubes rather than people. It's so different now, I've been called single minded but is that a compliment? Let's hope so.

The image on the facing page was inspired by the theme 'shadows'. It's one of my favourites and is taken outside a famous landmark close to Bath's City Centre; I am pleased with it in particular because if you look closely you will see not just my shadow but a couple with their shadows and also the shadow of trees in the grounds of this building. I don't know who said "no man is an island" but the news at the moment is all about Great Britain becoming independent of imported gas and oil by putting up more sustainable wind farms. Do the numbers add up though? There are around 65 million people in the United Kingdom all cooking lunch at around the same time. It's a big dream but should we really be cutting ourselves off from the rest of the world especially at a time when most of our manufacturing is done overseas? I am not really high minded, it's many years since I wrote to my MP or the Prime Minister, we have no say and my other sister thinks it was Mark Twain who said "if voting changed anything they'd ban it". But there's no denying that no man is an island and we are becoming isolated after much talk about the 'global village'. So the shadows in my photograph are an allegory for the risk of too much isolation where our lives are reduced to shadows without the substance of human contact from the outside world.

Episode 3 - Kindness and Self Control

James 5: 7-8
Be patient, then, my brothers and sisters,
until the Lord comes. See how patient a farmer is
as he waits for his land to produce precious crops.
He waits patiently for the autumn and spring rains.
You also must be patient. Keep your hopes high,
for the day of the Lord's coming is near.

Harriet Beecher Stowe (1811-1896) was the author of "Uncle Tom's Cabin" published in 1852. She lived in the USA and campaigned against the atrocity of human slavery. The work was attributed to have sparked the American Civil War although there will have been many contributing factors. Stowe was a family matriarch but wrote other books and said "there is more done with pens than with swords". This was a message also attributed to the greatest letter writer of all - St Paul who spread a Christian message from a strong sense of calling.

In the first letter of St Paul to the Corinthians, Chapter 9 verses 24 to 27, he uses the analogy of a race. He says that the runners compete as if to win but only one can win the prize. But preparation for the race is a discipline of mind and body. This reminds me of arriving in College and our introduction was about seeking examination success. We were advised to aspire to score top marks in order to ensure we passed whereas if we only aimed for a pass our marks might go below what was required. I still use this principle today when I train for a sponsored walk like the one I took part in when I was working in the United States of America, detailed below.

Since returning to Bath, I have walked half of the Circuit of Bath Walk four times and three of those were clockwise. These walks are beautifully organised with a list of route instructions to follow. The one time I walked anti clockwise I remember coming through a boggy field as I approached a village centre and church where a surprisingly large, brown toad leapt out of the mud in front of me. I continued with my walk to a copse of trees then a style, after that it was all downhill to the Kennet and Avon Canal and a bus home. Walking clockwise on the other side of the City we would reach the summit of a local view point, then down again to the canal where I met with muse number 2 who was out stewarding the sponsored walk.

VIII.

ROBERT THE BRUCE

Episode 1 - Flesh or the Soul

James 1: 19-20
Remember this, my dear brothers and sisters!
Everyone must be quick to listen, but slow to speak
and slow to become angry. Human anger does not
achieve God's righteous purpose.

Many times have I heard these similar stories from school teachers always encouraging their eager flock to persevere and continue to try without giving up. The message is 'if at first you don't succeed, try, try again'. The ancient legend of Robert the Bruce tells of his defeat in battle then his withdrawal alone into the shelter of a cave. At the entrance, or mouth of the cave our hero saw a spider weaving its web. Everything the wind and rain blew against the spider made the creature just keep on going until the beautiful, lacy filigree web was finished. Robert the Bruce realised that he must regroup his troops and stand against adversity one more time. Then the battle was won and our hero crowned King of Scotland.

For many years I have enjoyed taking part in sponsored walks for charity and got involved with the Crop Walk in aid of the hungry, when I was in San Antonio, Texas. There was a whole group of people taking part from my local church and we started by driving to the South of the City where there was a Riverwalk past the old Mission

Churches. The churches dated back to the Spanish Conquistadors of the 16th Century and had a simple design with a bell tower or Campanile.

Once we had parked, we walked three miles alongside the San Antonio River on a perfect, spring day when the Texas State Flower, the Bluebonnet, was blooming by the roadsides. In that part of Texas it would start to warm up in April then get very hot until the rains in September when it would thunder. The walk was completed by returning upstream to our cars so the total walk was six miles and there were three churches. I raised almost a hundred dollars and posted a cheque to the Crop Walk Head Office.

Not long after the sponsored walk we celebrated Easter then I returned to the United Kingdom and eventually came back to domicile in Bath once again.

Episode 2 - Seeking Contentment

Matthew 6: 19-21
"Do not store up riches for yourselves here on earth,
where moths and rust destroy, and robbers break in
and steal. Instead, store up riches for yourselves in
heaven, where moths and rust cannot destroy,
and robbers cannot break in and steal.
For your heart will always be
where your riches are".

A ROLE FOR ALL

For the work of Christian service
Our God gave gifts to all
That each might find fulfilment
One body, one spirit, one Lord.

We have a special duty
Our gifts for everyone
As no one is excluded
We've all had our race to run.

While some preach lovely stories
Our neighbours can explain
The others must be listening
To repeat this great refrain.

Beware deceit and rumour
Keep the body clean
For love came down from Heaven
That at the last is seen.

This above poem is inspired by the letter of St Paul to the Ephesians and it's a favourite passage of mine because it tells us that everyone has a part to play. St Paul also compares the church of God to the human body which has many parts all needing the other parts.

Episode 3 - Some Ups, Some Downs

T.S. Eliot (1885 - 1965)
From Journey of the Magi.
Then at dawn we came down to a temperate valley,
Wet, below the snow line, smelling of vegetation,
With a running stream and a water-mill
beating the darkness,
And three trees on the low sky.

Bath is a temperate valley but around me the grass is very brown today after a long, hot spell with only a short shower. I was reminded of a hot summer a long time ago when a friend of mine suggested lunch. He wanted a lager shandy for refreshment so I reserved a table at a City Centre cafe that was licensed. It was the hottest day of the year, everybody else headed for the beach or the park and the restaurant was deserted. The manager said "you can have any table you like", so my spoiled friend said to me "why did you reserve a table?" Well, you can see that it didn't last.

But it was a very different story when muse number three took me to a posh vegetarian restaurant and made the reservation himself. We dined in great style, had a seat by an open window looking out onto the garden then finished with coffee in the Parade Gardens al fresco. This friendship lasted ten years and was only ended by the separation of the Covid pandemic which meant that we had to remain two metres apart in the Salisbury Cathedral shop and couldn't shake hands or hug. What a wonderful, darling man.

Today (June 15th 2023) it's not as hot as yesterday but my smart phone tells me that thunder and rain is coming on Sunday 18th.

IX.

ETERNAL JOY

Episode 1 - Pandora's Box

Luke 17: 5-6
The apostles said to the Lord, "Make our faith greater."
The Lord answered, "If you had faith as big as
a mustard seed, you could say to this mulberry tree,
'Pull yourself up by the roots and plant yourself
in the sea!' and it would obey you."

The image on the facing page shows a yellow flower called Nemesia, that I grew from seed on my window sill. It is a wonderful, restorative feeling to grow a plant and this year I will be sowing sweet peppers and Cauliflower to see if I can grow these vegetables to use in cooking. The herbs were a great success in previous times; I used coriander in salsas and I added this herb to rice when serving a curry. My late mother loved lilac so she planted a tree in the garden of the house I grew up in. It took a number of years to flower but once it did there were the most abundant blooms year on year attracting the bees but also the neighbourhood children. They would reach over the fence to take some flowers but my memory suggests that there were still plenty left. We also grew a flowering, grass like plant that Mam called Monbretia although she did say it tended to take over.

It's so true that children grow up to fly the nest but can still need their parents. I was 25 years old when I had my wisdom teeth out as described above. My mother really was like a pelican that feeds its young from its own breast. My depression started to kick in about that time and my mother came to my home again for a few days to keep me company over the weekend.

Although the disparity some people insist exists between religion and science has never bothered me, it seems that great thinkers are still visiting this question today. Biblically, sickness was attributed to sin or wrongdoing while so-called insanity was thought to be due to the possession of demons. We know that nowadays science has more logical explanations such as a biochemical imbalance, faulty gene or infection but both sides of the argument can be equally entrenched. My mother did not apportion blame and had a good capacity to see the bigger picture.

My late father did not achieve legal custody of the family, it was always seen as a mother's role in those days, but he did have access and took me on cycling holidays across the length of Great Britain. We visited Snowdonia, the Peak District, Shropshire, Edinburgh and Glasgow. We stayed in youth hostels which in those days were good value with self catering facilities. It was hugely inspiring and we talked to the very end of the man we met in Chester who said "it's all part of the rich tapestry of life". Cycling into Perth I had a puncture and a German couple popped me into the back of their Campervan until we caught up with Dad. He insisted on fixing the puncture then the following day we were riding over the Forth Road Bridge downhill into Edinburgh via Queensferry Road.

Dad also took me to see Macbeth in Stratford upon Avon and during that holiday we visited Coventry Cathedral which was the only trip he went with me inside a church. We saw the ceiling high tapestry at the east end and the contemporary etchings on the vast, glass wall at the west front. In later years when I'd given up cycling my father kept up the activity with his second partner who he met on holiday in the Lake District. Then he did come to church with me at Llandaff Cathedral, Westminster Abbey and in his own local church in Yorkshire where his ashes now rest. It is a lovely location in the Vale of York and it is a Saxon church.

Episode 2 - Avoiding Isolation

Matthew 28: 5-7
The angel spoke to the women. "You must not be afraid,"
he said. "I know you are looking for Jesus,
who was crucified. He is not here; he has been raised,
just as he said. Come here and see the place where
he was lying. Go quickly now, and tell his disciples,
'He has been raised from death, and now he is going
to Galilee ahead of you; there you will see him!'
Remember what I have told you."

Isolation has been an issue in my life as when I became too unwell to work in the field of medical research I lost contact with all but two former colleagues. I was discharged from the psychiatric unit in Bath and went home with nothing to do and nowhere to go. There was no discharge plan and no follow up. So I phoned the unit to ask if there was anything they could suggest and the day centres were recommended to me. I joined and became a long standing member, and eventually there were newsletters I could write for as well as craft groups finally resulting in my setting up a peer support group called the Bath Survivors Network. The group enjoyed a trip to Prior Park Landscape Garden, a visit to the Pump Rooms for morning coffee and a few meetings of planning with off loading. We disbanded but some of us left to play bowls in a more inclusive group and my writing became more important.

The worst aspect of a severe mental illness can be that it's invisible. But I found that being obese and having no offspring, both very visible problems, caused me more adverse judgement than the diagnosis of mental health. I have a double whammy with an ovarian cyst that had to be removed. But most ordinary folk are more accepting and the worst discrimination came when I achieved recovery because it's hard for new people I meet to recognise that I was very unwell only five years ago. Some health care professionals say that my diagnosis was "a long time ago". It's a pointless comment because if it is a biochemical imbalance then it is there for life. You could argue that writing is a lone job but I have met people through selling books and attending courses both at the day centre as well as our local College.

The quote at the head of this section is the story of the first Easter morning when the risen Jesus revealed himself to a woman. We like to think that the Lord did much to empower the women around him and I found a new acceptance recently that I had not known in the past.

Episode 3 - In Life We Trust

1 Thessalonians 5: 16-22
Be joyful always, pray at all times,
be thankful in all circumstances.
This is what God wants from you in your life
in union with Christ Jesus.
Do not restrain the Holy Spirit;
do not despise inspired messages.
Put all things to the test; keep what is good
and avoid every kind of evil.

BY THE LAKE

Here the sound of water soothes
Babbling, trickling, pouring down
Robin red breast darts amongst
Leaves or berries, nature's wine

Peace is in a garden fair
Eden found before the Fall
'Neath a sturdy pergola
Festooned with roses, verdure, calls

The wild, the lost, a chance to breathe
How will I remember thee?
As a gardener of the soul
Or a life buoy out to sea.

I think that the most important quote in this whole of my memoir is the one for Episode 3 of story IX; be thankful in all circumstances. It is not always as easy to do as it is to affirm. The photograph is one of our City Centre parks where there is a sensory garden in remembrance of King

George VI (1895-1952). This is a beautiful, tranquil oasis of calm in the midst of all the hustle and bustle where I sometimes sit with a bottle of water to relax before an important appointment and to think through everything I plan to talk or write about. It's soothing, it's enjoyable to see the children spotting goldfish and it gives me a chance to sit quietly before dealing with anything stressful. This is my favourite photo out of all the ones I've taken because you can see the water, the reflection and the water lilies. Claude Monet would have been in his element! In the height of summer the pergolas are smothered in climbing roses in full bloom, white with double petals and characteristic pointed, green leaves. The stems are old and very woody yet the flowers come back year on year for as long as I can remember which is 34 years.

To conclude part 1 then I would say for the third time "be thankful in all circumstances" and count your blessings.

TREASURE WITHIN
Part 2

POETRY

TREASURE WITHIN PART 2
CONTENTS

Mementoes in Verse

Reflections of Time

When Summer Comes
Languor
The Stonemason's Art
Glorious Isolation
Homeward Bound
An Advantage
A Tidy Cawl!
Thoughts On A Lost Muse
Speaking Silence
In Honey Coloured Stone
Free Will
A Homecoming
The Sick Friend
A Prayer For Well-being

Doodles, Dog Ears and Ditties

If Stones Could Speak
The Avenue
Refresh, Revive, Renew
The Waning Moon
Night Time Reflection
Baking Bread
To Music
Our First Meeting
Sandcastles
The Flight of Steps
Glasgow City
Bookmarks
A Pentecostal Prayer For Profit
The Mysterious Monster of Midsomer Madness
Ansaphone
H2O

A Boy's Anthem

A Beautiful Game
A Seagull's Song
As Petals Fall
Immortality
Radiant Fire And Translucent Flame
With Golden Glow
Evergreen
In Perfect Harmony
My Gift to You
Reversi
The Elf King's Dream
Waters Meet
The Pen Pixie
Centenary
Feel the Pulse
The Guns Were Stilled
On Coventry Cathedral
Flights of Fancy
Sweet Maytime
Bluebell Woods
Bowls Night
Lines For St Faith's Chapel, Westminster Abbey
The Volunteer

Mementoes in Verse

BECAUSE YOU'RE YOU

Because you're you I love you
Because you're you I care
I'll walk along beside you
My life with you I'll share

Should you be any different
I'd love you still the same
You are my joy my one desire
'Twas dark before you came

Because you're you there's roses
On every leafy tree
Will you be mine for always
And give your love to me?

For when the darkness takes me
My body will be cold
But I'll be there beside you
My love will not grow old.

FOOD FOR THOUGHT

We're out here and it's freezing
The duckling must be cold
I'll have her baked for supper
Before I'm very old

Oh sweet and lovely duckling

So good with cherry sauce
I'll warm you in the oven
I will feel no remorse

Your botty must be freezing
Your wings must be quite chapped
We'll sort you out in no time
Before you feel relapsed

So tasty, meaty duckling
Let's eat and eat tonight
We'll dine on mash and carrots
And warm you up just right.

A SPOKEN HYMN

Lord of all Earth and the Heavens and the Firmament
Creator and maker, sustainer all permanent
Guide us this day, lead us always;
Teach the Good News and the glory for aye.

Praise every dew drop, each flower and each element
Sing to the Lord giving thanks for the day.
Let faith be strong, keep hope along
Trust in His grace and His mercy so sure.

We who are helpless, so small and so hesitant,
Put all our trust in the Father of Abraham
God of our ancestors, King of salvation
Lead us each moment to thy divine throne

Make every mountain, the rivers, the ocean wide
Speak out his constancy over our time and tide
Sing of His love, praise One above

Tell of His glory for all of our lives

Lord of all Earth and the Heavens and the Firmament
Creator and Maker, sustainer all permanent
Guide us this day, lead us always
Teach the Good News and the glory for aye.

I HEREBY RESOLVE.....

I hereby resolve...

That when push comes to shove, I'll fight like a man
If patience allows I'll give in when I can

Should the lightning crash and the thunder roar
I'll build a big boat though waters should pour

If money comes to me I'll give some away
But keep just a little for that rainy day

When trouble occurs I'll meet it halfway
Should love touch my shoulder
I'll not go astray

If you cannot find me I'm here on the phone
With our constant friendship we're never alone

So here's to the New Year what luck will it bring?
Some fame or some fortune
Some losses, some wins
Whatever life holds from this moment forth
I hereby resolve to take the bull by the horns!

LET TRUMPETS SOUND

Hark, the bugles bright and blazing
See the bride so white and dazzling
Softly spoken vows endearing
Golden ring of love exchanging
Music fills the church with song
Crowds are gathered, a hearty throng.

Spirits rise she is so lovely
Groom beside her, smart and comely
Tears of joy then smiles of laughter
Champagne sparkles ever after
Marks the dawn of fairy tale
Kate and William, your big day.

Viewed by all who wish you well
Pomp and beauty, glories tell
Of the love you both will share
For the roles you both will wear.

SHIFTING SANDS

Paddling on the beach at Weymouth Bay
The sands beneath my feet, the tide holds sway
Seagulls swoop and storm clouds shade the day
Your hand in mine, you turn to me and say
That in your heart a secret must unfold
To let me know the oldest story told
You love me as no other ever could
We share a single dream and if I should
But only whisper "Dear I love you true",
Then you will be my guide and constant star
And I will be forever in your care.

Paddling every mile of Weymouth Beach
Your hand and heart are never out of reach
For should I grow too old for happy pleasures
This moment is a day I'll always treasure.
So, keeping you in mind this sunny day
Remember me whatever comes your way
For you and I will always be together
Through rain and shine, through sun and stormy weather.

THE ROSE

Dark Rose of Lancashire
From forces moved to Wales
Repose in sleep, your work all done
Six lovely children and I am one
Who always will remember.

You taught me everything I know
The names of flowers and trees,
Your guidance gives a power of thought
Love's influence a steady hand
Worth more than precious gold.

Dear Mam we travelled to the beach
And paddled in the sea
We saw a heron and a hawk
Took boat trips out across the bay
And journeyed on life's stony way.

If time when passed should cause us both
To meet again at last
I'd tell you Mam how well you've done
And hold our memories fast.

TO FATHER

He has the wisdom of his years
That I will yet achieve
His sense of humour sees him through
But he does not believe.

He loves his Opera, brews his wine
He cycles far and near
On memories he loves to dwell
Of all that he holds dear

He often speaks about the War
Its bloodshed and its pain
It is my very fervent prayer
We see it not again

If I could give a gift to him
It would be something small
A token of my great esteem
To reunite us all.

THE BILLS, THE BILLS

There was a time in days of old
When bills fell on the mat
They'd come at once
In droves of three
Each quarter oh so regularly
Demanding payment instantly
For heating and all that.

Chorus:.   The bills, the bills, the dreaded bills
            Four awful times a year
            No respite from their cold demand
            No comfort and no cheer

Now modern times are here at last
The paying is done for you
It's all precisely computerised
With monthly payments from you
Directly, neatly debited you do not stop to think
No need to save, no hassle or worry
Just as long as you've got the money

Chorus

The price of fuel's gone sky high
The cost of water's soaring
The World is coming to an end
The sky is almost falling.
Pockets are empty, smiles are thin
We're struggling every day
But others much less fortunate
No rainfall comes their way

Chorus

Where trees and livestock fail to thrive
Where drought, disease prevail
Where people starve and need our help
Let's pray for them today.

Chorus:.   The bills, the bills, the dreaded bills
            Four awful times a year
            No respite from their cold demand
            No comfort and no cheer.

THE RUBBISH DUMP

I am a great believer
In throwing things away
It's past it's useful sell by date
It can no longer stay

My friend he is a hoarder
A pack rat some would say
He'll keep it all
What's big and small
Whatever comes his way

He calls it "come in useful",
Or "handy someday soon";
That broken chair, that leaky mug
That bent and battered spoon.

Each piece will tell a story
Of how it had its day
The memory of all the times
It came in use, some way.

He says the same of people
The poor, the rich, them all
Each one has different stories
Much know-how great and small.

Do not discard the people
Because they've had their day
Their value is immeasurable
Their worth is here to stay.

I am a great believer

In keeping for the best
Those friends and family dear to me
That make up for all the rest.

So treasure all the people
Who come your way through life
But if you feel you disagree
Then listen to them carefully
They may be in the right.

To end this potent lecture
I will be heard to say:-
"I'll treasure words of love and care,
And chuck the rest away."

FOR SHIRLEY, OR...AN ODE TO EATING FISH.

Young Shirley tasted every dish
But turned her nose up at the fish,
The salmon, trout, cod, skate or bream
Would make poor Shirley shout and scream

"I will not eat this muck", cried she
"It makes me heave and then you'll see
I turn a nasty colour green
Because I find it quite obscene".

Stepped in a dietician bold
"Young Shirley, if you will grow old
You need your mackerel, tuna, plaice
Or else your heart will run its race.

A diet strict I'll make you eat,
Cod liver oil and pills complete

And while you're at it take some tea,
It's full of antioxidants, see".

We'll Shirley tried it for a while
She popped the pills and supped the oil
But soon she started to rebel
And then we heard her start to tell.

"Oh fiendish Miss Nutritionist
Just stop a mo and tell me this-
If fish is meant to make you clever,
Why didn't Einstein live forever?"

The dietician rolled her eyes
And held her hands up to the skies
"Oh Shirley, Shirley for pity's sake!
Can I not tempt you with some hake?

There's haddock, halibut and sole
Try scampi, shark or sturgeon's roe,
You will feel better I am sure
And cease to make such a furore".

Young Shirl went home to do some cooking
But soon as fiendish nurse stopped looking
She fed the haddock to the cat
Who licked her chops, well fancy that.

The moral to this fishy tale
Is, if you're partial to sperm whale
It may not be the cup of tea
For others, like our young Shirley.

A CHRISTMAS KISS

Sshh! Sshh! Don't say a word now
The children are in bed
The fire is dying down now
Peace reigns in our homestead

Dear love for just one moment
Share a Christmas kiss with me
The mistletoe is hanging
Beside the sparkling tree

Another year is over
Of happiness and bliss
So spend some time with me now
And share that Christmas kiss.

BEFORE THE DAWN

Time marked by the ticking of a clock
Creeps slowly towards the delayed daylight
Late on a winter's morn

Sleep is over
Too soon for comfort
The sounds of distant traffic
Herald a city's gradual awakening

A realisation, centuries old
That amidst the glitz and glamour
Of "jingle bells" and tinsel
A child is on His way

Too soon, I am not ready

Too late, I did not hear the high plaintive cry
The clarion call to worship.
A bell tolls and
In all this preparation
I spare a thought for children
Born in poverty today,

A thousand lives touched by
The love of God
Frail as I am
I serve when I can.

CARDIFF BAY

Tides out, mud in charge
Birds swoop, worms duck
Old supermarket trollies
Litter the stinking flats
Decayed buildings
Closed church
Red brick and pier head
Custom House and bank counter
Memories lost
Forgotten era.

Coal and iron and steel
Ships and trade and commerce
Lost in time, all left behind
Industry marches on
Thriving, bustling dock
Stands as still as stone
Dirty water, pools of oil
All that's left of human toil
The excrement of labour.

Renovate, replenish, restore
A barrage, a lake, a wall
Freshwater fish
Ice cream in tubs
A cafe, a hotel
Theatre and song
Words in Welsh
Bronze and slate
A festival of fountains
A flotilla of craft.

Revitalise, renew
Re-open and re-use
Restaurants, museums
Leisure and pleasure
Cruises across the Bay
A footpath, a journey, a stay
All welcome, all for the day
Refreshment, fulfilment
Find sanctuary at the Bay.

A BOAT TRIP

Darling I dreamt we took the boat
Along the River of Life
We met on the shore, you opened a door -
I want to be your wife.

Sweetheart the boat was a sturdy craft
A barge of metal and steel
The rudder was sturdy, conditions set fair
I thought we were in it for real.

Dearest, a storm brewed up that night
A storm of menace and might
The boat overturned, our ship ran aground
We were swept from each other
I'd lost my dear lover
My friend was gone from my sight.

Honey tonight my thoughts lie with you
So near, yet so far and now gone
If you I could reach, my feelings I'd preach
'Till I could convince you we're one.

Beloved I'm building a craft tonight
A ship of passion and love
And over the water my words will not falter
As I tremblingly send you a dove.

My pigeon of peace, a bird without price
Is winging its way to you soon
Accept my enquiry and get out your diary
And meet by the light of the moon.

Darling I dreamt we took the boat
Along the River of Life
We'll meet by the shore and for richer or poor
My sweetheart, I'll be your wife.

DISPARITY?

We have diverse encounters
Two very different kinds
You've worked so hard, I've been so I'll
I talk to you, the magic spell
Unfolds and I unwind.

Well versed on many issues
That we discuss so free
We'll chat about my mental health
Such topics ranging from a wealth
Of what our tastes agree.

My future will get covered
We won't neglect the past
With you the darkness comes to light
I feel relief, so cleansed and bright
I want it so to last.

You say you're in your fifties
I'm only forty one
Not conscious of a stumbling block
It doesn't come as such a shock
Our journey's never done.

We've come from different places
We meet with health in mind
It is so good to talk it through
I relish moments spent with you
I'm cheered and I unwind.

COMMUNITY SUPPORT, MARIA SPEAKING

She owns a floating vessel
A dog called boatswain too
She's lived abroad as she will tell
As she's supporting you.

Maria's blonde and feisty
Political with vigour

Each task she takes on daily
Approaching it with rigour.

Athletic and so sporty
She'll walk and talk and swim
She'll be there should you need it
If you're out on a limb.

To write about Maria
And do her justice fair
Is not an easy task I'd say
So I will leave it there.

ON SOLITUDE

In my rooms I dwell
With music and with thought
My poems do console me
Making 'phone calls lifts me
I think I'll have more tea.

In the park I stroll
Avoiding dogs and kids
The cyclists do annoy me
The tourists they enrage me
I think I'll have more tea.

I'm here at the canal
The boats so gay and free
The people wave and chat
The locks so deep and cold
A great place to grow old
I think I'll have more tea.

Now the Garden Centre
From rain it shelter's me
The plants are blooming lovely
The cards are dear but pretty
Oh great! They're serving tea.

At last I'm home once more
Happy, weary and foot sore
A nap will now refresh me
A drink it will restore me
Let's have that cup of tea.

THE CHANGING SEASONS

Each morning there's dew on the grass
It's fresh as a daisy, the daylight is rosy
The flowers appearing, the lambs so endearing
It's spring and it comes round so fast.

In summer the rain is so cool
My spirits embrace it's touch on my face
The green things do flourish, the Earth it will nourish
I relish its drops on the pool.

With autumn comes frost on the leaf
The colours are changing, the stags they are rutting
The squirrels are hunting for nuts they are storing
It's lovely but oh it's so brief.

It's winter and winds they do blow
The Sun will not show, the plants will not grow
It's dark very soon, with never a moon
There's Christmas but then there's no snow.

But when the New Year rushes in
With parties and drinking, with singing and eating
The spring will be here, we love it so dear
We know that it's not long to go.

WARD ROUND WINDOW

I love him, he loves his job
He'll call he says at 6 o'clock
For I am waiting in my frock
But will it last for always?

6.55 and I will chance
The no.19 bleep
He answers but I have to wait
For busy doctor's running late
The War Round lasts for always.

At last we meet, I'm tired and cross
We head straight for the pub
You're worth your weight in gold because
You don't get mad, you keep your cool
The memory lasts for always.

If I could have you back again
I'd only change one thing
I'd read a book, I'd bake a cake
'Till midnight would I calmly wait
And I'd be yours for always.

WET SUMMER 2007

They say the rain is here to stay
'Till autumn comes once more
They say it's wetter than each year
That ever went before.

Preceded by a dry, dry spring
So long, so hot and then
The rain it never seems to cease
Not now, not here but when?

The days are dark and cloudy
There's drizzle on the grass
It's been like this for weeks now
It never seems to pass.

The tennis was a wash out
The cricket's gone to tea
They say it's worse in Belfast
But that's not helping me.

If only it was sunny
Between the drops of rain
We'd all go out in sunshine
And then we'd smile again!

Reflections of Time

REFLECTIONS OF TIME

Can we control you?
Dare we extol you?
Should we uphold you?
Will we ignore you?
Yours is the final say.

A moment, a day, a year
A lifetime, an epoch, an era
Too trifling to count, a piffling amount
Consider my time as a chimaera.

The camera records each age
With pictures for every stage
All faded and brown
An image of town
When corsets and hoops were the rage.

Come closer to hear what I say
Please love me for more than one day
Will you keep me near
For all of the year
As clocks tick our heartbeats away?

Enjoy every moment we spend
Dear loving and all faithful friend
Eternally young, our song have I sung
As ditties and chants have I penned.

We look to the end of all time
The fruit of celestial vine

When woe is all gone
Let this be our song -
"My darling, oh will you be mine?"

PUBLIC TRANSPORT

It might be every hour
It could be once a day
It's not enough, it's cause for shame
And we don't have a say

The managers they tell us
We don't use it enough
But can you really blame us
When waiting is so tuff?

It's tardy if it's running
It's cancelled if not late
Will I get stuck in Welshpool?
Or make it home by 8?

Leaves on the line or traffic
Excuses all are there
To stray from home is risky
Go further if you dare!

I'm tired and tired of waiting
All passengers beware
It is a National scandal
Take action Mister Blair!

CHEATING TIME

Can I cheat time?
Or does time cheat me?
At the bus stop
Neon signs mock
Bus is due, bus is due
Ten years later
What else is new?

Long delays and endless traffic
Clock watch impatience
Solves nothing
Dragging time is cheating me
Why this endless hour of lifetime?
Lasting 'till the end of never

Morning comes, we meet at last
Two hours never went so fast
Several coffees slowly sipped
Wow, is that the time? We quip

Finally the nights are drawing
Sleep comes soothing, soft and slow
Seconds later sees the daybreak
Did I cheat time?
How could I though?

With the dawning of a new day
Back to board the tardy bus
Could I only cheat my calendar
I would spend my life as us.

THE HUMAN CONDITION

Our lives are so brief
But whilst we are here
We must cherish or hold
To all that is dear

So frail and so mortal
With strengths so untried
We love one another
For He who has died

In truth does He lead us
As we can aspire
To greater new effort
Whenever we tire

With challenge comes triumph
With failures come tears
We take it more lightly
With passing of years

With flaws in our make-up
Temptations within
Hold fast to conviction
Find freedom from sin.

IS IT YOU?

I come to browse and here I pause
Each photo' smiling, happy, gay;
This time I thought I'd stop to look
And for a moment stop to pray.

Those sunny faces adorn the wall
Inside South Transept, behind choir stall;
They cheer my day, light up my way,
For everyone has a tale to say.

A gallery of Abbey staff
From high to low and all aglow,
Make visits worth a brief reflection
On all that's meaning in this direction.

You make my Sunday start aright
You're always there whate'er my plight;
I come and go but you're immutable
The worth of you is indisputable.

So keep my senses, my spirits floating
Pursue this endeavour, ever lighting
Up our hearts and minds,
Inspiring, leading, mentored time.

IS IT ME?

Glory Lord, your voice is calling
Lilies bloom then fade and die
Cheer me Lord, responses falling
Hear my answer to your cry

I am mute but ever yearning
In my heart a constant burning
Always with me as I pray
Be my guide throughout the day

Voices in the Market Square
It's you, it's you, you're always there

I am feeble, humble, frail
Yet I seek your Holy Grail

Call again for I am ready
My heart is strong, it's beat is steady
Where I go I cannot tell
You're beside me, all is well.

WHEN SUMMER COMES

Take a walk with God the while
Over hedge and over style
See the beauty there before
Flowers and blossoms, leaves galore

Leave your earnest cares behind
Out of sight and out of mind
Reach for solace, ask for love
Look for signs of God above

Keep your thoughts in tune with Nature
Feel the gentle loss of pressure
Let your body and soul rejoice
Feel the spirit, hear the voice

Bring back friends you can recall
Speak of love to one and all
Let your Maker hear your story
Seek His counsel, share His glory

End your walk refreshed and still
Find repose for then you will
Tackle troubles as they come
'Till your earthly race is run.

LANGUOR

A pleasant state
Me and my mate
In dreamy mode
Relaxing in style
Like two turtle doves
Just once in a while
On a distant beach
Your arms within reach
Just pass me the wine
And chocolates, divine.

Oh wow did you hear?
The radio's near
Our favourite song
It went on so long
Oh sweet, darling muse
Don't ever confuse
This passion I feel
With anything real.

THE STONEMASON'S ART

Ripples, circles, waves or beams
Angles, joints and seamless seams
One false move the whole erupts
Stones that stand like emblems plucked
From minds affixed on God

Vaulting blooms like Easter lilies
Fountains built to move the heart

One line pillar, staunch colossus
Holds the roof boss, strokes the stars

Tracery like finest lace
Sharp with detail, kingly face
Looks upon the throng below
Calmed by candles' eerie glow

Time stands still, I gaze in wonder
Taken down the paths once trod
By the years of ceaseless worship
Keep our minds affixed on God.

For the Chapter House of Wells Cathedral.

GLORIOUS ISOLATION

Found alone in glorious isolation
With you oh Lord, help is at hand
My footsteps may falter
My burden may burn
Ever you are near me
From you may I learn
The path to see clearly
In darkness or day
The road stretched before me
The truth and the way

No loneliness haunts me
With you close at hand
Your comfort shall guide me
Mere mortal I am
For as the light brightens
And morning is near

Immeasurable comfort
Pours out as I hear
Your voice and direction
Though strife grieves me sore
Oh Lord my redeemer
Now and evermore.

HOMEWARD BOUND

I am born without awareness
I am young and unfulfilled
My needs and wants are met
More food, more love and yet
My spirit won't be stilled

My growth is fast and urgent
No curb restrains it's pace
Youth will not last, will soon be past
For now I run its race

I am a learned equal
With books I prosper well
My work takes on new meaning
With which to cast my spell

The time came when I met you
A cherished moment sweet
Let's keep together, in every weather
See sunshine as we greet

Today we are much older
Companions dear and close
For you I'd turn the angry tide
Split forth the river deep and wide

To prove you're loved the most
Your home is in my heart dear
My home is where you dwell

To be with you is soothing
My love a sturdy shell
This world is only fleeting
We all must needs move on
But should I see you after
I'll meet with you in rapture
When strife and woe are gone.

AN ADVANTAGE

I stop awhile to pause and pray
For this is how I live today
A character that's built on books
Worth more than money, goods or looks

For reading is a perfect pleasure
And writing is it's perfect foil
If I could change my life's endeavour
I'd never swap my daily toil

Young people be prepared for action
Take heart and learn while chance prevails
For as you grow you'll find direction
From classics, literature and tales

Your studies take imagination
Beyond the flight of all things known
As knowledge builds of our creation
You'll travel far beyond your home

To your advantage then this learning
And to your wealth such gifts expand
For as your journey is progressing
More gifts enrich as life unfolds

With diligence to persevere
The Universe takes shape at last
With every word to reach my ear
I hold great wisdom in my grasp

To you my teacher all rejoicing
Such pleasant and rewarding tasks
Maybe for always to your praises
We hope your spirit ever lasts.

A TIDY CAWL!

Its proper Cawl, it's not just stew
For this is what you have to do:-
Put carrots, parsnips, spuds and swede
Put onion, shin beef, leeks and stock
Cook slowly in the melting pot
Then after several hours have past
You'll find you eat the wholesome lot!

It's made for sharing, be not sparing
The flavour floods as Cawl doth simmer
But live on this and you'll be trimmer
Not fattening, wicked, sinful, bad
It keeps the winter out when sad.
So make the Cawl and make it tidy
And keep leftover bits 'till Friday
And if still peckish make some more-
It really is a treat galore!

THOUGHTS ON A LOST MUSE

Oh gentle muse so good and true
You came into my life
Such inspiration drawn from you
With colours bold of every hue
And shades of day and night

Your peaceful message calms my soul
With songs and words of love
For though you're gone, you are my all
You charmed my mind, kept me in thrall
And kept my spirit bright

Oh faithless muse restore my heart
Be loving, kind and sweet
Or else move on and leave my brain
Another friend to greet.

SPEAKING SILENCE

Speaking sounds enthral my ear
No rest, no quiet within
The gulls are nesting
Sirens screaming
Engines running
Never still

The hurly burly of my life
While rushing here and there
Leaves just a corner in the strife
To say a word of prayer

I turn to you my Lord, in prayer
To find the stillness resting there
For here at last is peace revealed
The noises and the sounds are stilled

A quiet moment in my room
Makes every trouble settle
Alone with you in time and space
I feel the warmth of love's embrace
Oh silence precious ever

The silence of an empty church
The peace of love revealed
For someday soon I'm on my way
My song of love now healed.

IN HONEY COLOURED STONE

Sunrise lights a quiet city
Warm pink tones refresh the sky
Seagulls wake, invoking freedom
Morning coffee, papers hard by

Slowly traffic builds awakening
Colours vibrant greet the eye
Honey coloured Doric pillars
Line my street by river's side

Warm in daylight, cream with ginger
Biscuit flavoured sandstone carved
Pediments above the pavements
Ancient notions, noble baths

Sunset late on summer's evening
Lifts the valley's honeyed hue
All the hills around will savour
Riches cast as quarry hewn.

FREE WILL

An uncontested right for all
Confined and checked by Law
Our liberty we take as read
'Til lost its cherished more

I choose my clothes, my friends, my food
I'll walk where're I may
But others not so fortunate
Forswear the light of day

Trapped in a prison of the mind
So many years sedated
Deprived of work and company
Alone and isolated

I would not have it thus if I
Could change the world and make
The standards which the people set
Provide more give and take

You feel forlorn as if you've failed
Yourself and others too
But with free will you can see change
And to yourself be true

I did not wish it on myself
It came not of my choice

But with free will now I can yield
My power and my voice.

A HOMECOMING

I travelled the world, my secret dream
To see its scenes unfold
A restless spirit searching yet
To find that pot of Gold

I found the values that I held
Were all around and set
By all the nations steadfastly
In perfect unanimity
With everyone I met

The beauties of this lovely Earth
No tongue can ever tell
A feast for eyes and ears and smell
With people that I love so well
A glorious growing old

But greener than the deepest dye
This land called Wales is mine
And if one day I should return
It surely must of all the lands
Be where I'd choose to die

So welcome me oh Land of Song
And open up your heart
I'll rest with you, and I'll be true
I swear we'll never part.

THE SICK FRIEND

I've walked so many weary miles
My boots are worn to shreds
My feet are sore, the Sun beats down
But on my journey I reflect
On all that matters most

The river runs around my feet
My arms are stretched out wide
I drink with pleasure, swim for fun
I dream of drowning in its life
Its water cleanses me of strife
I feel its potent power

My homeward trek fulfils my soul
I tread with joyous step
To see your face, to hear your voice
Light up as I lift up our cup
And to your lips the water press
Is worth a pot of gold

For here I am at journey's end
And here's to you my worthy friend
Let's eat and drink together
For you are mine and we will dine
In Paradise 'till end of time
Our love will last forever.

A PRAYER FOR WELL-BEING

Dear Lord

May the rain never cease upon my face
May the Sun always tell of your Grace

Let the Earth yield its riches evermore
May my life ever respond to your call

May my heart always warm to the needy
May my mind be alert, bold and strong

Let the fields, flowers and skies ever feed me
With the spiritual vision of your song

May my will ever move to your tuning
May my craft ever write what you will

For when the day dawns I stop singing
May I meet you at last and be still.

Doodles, Dog Ears and Ditties

IF STONES COULD SPEAK

An island bathed in summer sun
A rock beset by storms
I battled bravely, wind and wave
The rain beats down
The wind is cold.

No shelter here, no nook or cranny
My feet are numb
My shoulders hunched
I am as fixed as stone.

Before me ground as fine as dust
A million grains of sand,
My certain fate as time moves on
To yield to times as fortune deals
This rock, a changing hand.

If stones could speak, I'd tell my tale
Of peoples that passed by
A dozen shipwrecks at my door
And happy picnics on the shore
Of children playing, lovers meeting
Rock pools filled with life galore
But I am as fixed as stone.

THE AVENUE

Cherry trees form a line of sheer beauty
Straight and true with blossoms frothy pink
They mark a path from end to end
Planted many years ago and thriving ever since.

I walk this path alone all times of year
I see the golds of autumn and leaf fall
In winter branches bare berate the sky
As if to ask our maker Why, oh why?

Spring comes with warmer days and cheery song
The ice is melting, buds are bursting forth
Days draw longer, starry skies at night
The cuckoo's song is heard, now winged in flight.

The Avenue is pink as once before
The gardens spring to life as waters flow
My life shrugs off its winter coat of woe
For happy times return to me once more.

REFRESH, REVIVE, RENEW

Drink, oh water living life force
Refresh my body, quench my thirst
Ever new and always circling
Dew drops fall as morning breaks

Eventide, my spirits flagging
Revive my soul, oh earthly spring
Bathe my aching limbs and members
Rejoice with every living thing

Baptise this frail and mortal body
Cleanse my heart from thoughts of sin
Bid me enter Salisbury's cloister
Keep me safe and warm within

Living water always moving
Ever new and ever young
Reflect my life before His altar
Renew my vows 'till senses dim

Floating, sinking, swimming, soaring
All sensations newly tried
Gaze in wonder, adoration
At this glorious Eastertide.

THE WANING MOON

Full for harvest, calm, serene
Moonbeams shine, unearthly gleam
Becoming slighter, moving tides
My heart beats faster
My arms held wide
Feel the shadows, long and yearning
Dusk to daylight, Earth stands turning

Welcomed every Eve at twilight
See the Moon rise o'er our lives
Now the new moon bringing luck
Open the window, do be quick
Turn the sixpence, make a wish
Sleep and dream of love's sweet kiss
Oh pale and lovely orb of light
Solace sought to soothe my plight.

NIGHT TIME REFLECTION

Twilight falls, as sadness dwells
With moments of reflection

The dying embers of the setting sun
Light up the West with orange hues
One lone star shines in the East
Then myriads come from far away
The plough, the bear, familiar shapes
Of Milky Way and stellar constellations

Sleep evades me on this night
Too hot for restful slumber
Have I done the right thing?
Could I have done more?
Did I say too much?
Should I eat my words?
What will become of me?

At last, repose and dreams of worry
Silly problems working through
Morning bringing kind solutions
Hope once more, I speak to you.

BAKING BREAD

It may be cold outside
But here it's hot as mustard
I'm kneading dough and warming yeast
With wholemeal flour I leave to rise
Beside the storage heater

It's such a warming feeling
To see the loaf come out
I breathe a sigh of such relief
It has doubled in size
All thanks to the storage heater

There's nothing left for me to do
But try it out with butter
It's light as air
It's fluffy inside
Well done, that storage heater

The oven takes some credit too
It should, of course, it's nearly new
The proof of the pudding is tucking in
I'm sorry, doc, I'll never be thin
I take my tea with bread and jam
Beside the storage heater

The weather's cold, the streets are as glass
The white stuff covers hedge and grass
But baking bread is breaking boredom
My loaf may not be set for stardom
But whilst I use it in this way
I'll live to bake another day
And warm myself from head to toe
Beside that storage heater.

TO MUSIC

Soothing, enchanting, uplifting
Played and loved for years
I feel sadness, gladness, joy
And shed many happy tears

Without my music I would lose
The solace of the night
When sleep evades me, darkness reigns
And other pleasures take flight

Gratitude I feel to those
Who practise such endeavour
To cheer my soul and lift my heart
In sun and stormy weather

The pleasures rich you give to me
I never shall repay
The concert ticket, small in price
Will end my weary day

Passion, pathos, all are there
With faith and fraud and folly
Some tunes are loud, some tunes are soft
Some sad and others jolly

At birth or death or all through life
You're there at every stage
May you always shine and live for aye
Enriching every age.

OUR FIRST MEETING

My nephew, warm and small in my lap
It's our first meeting, you're nine days old
Your little face puckers, you suck your sleeves
Needing food and a nap

You seem to respond to my gentle caress

You are so small and soft
Weighing in at just six pounds
You have character already

Suddenly, where did the years go?
You're roughly five years old
We're off to Castle Coch
In your makeshift car
Playing in the sunny garden

Now you're eighteen, doesn't time fly?
Geography is your endeavour
You'll fly the nest, you'll make new mates
But I'm Auntie, whatever the weather.

SANDCASTLES

With bucket and spade
In shallows we wade
Our shoulders so hot
With ankles so wet
For Summer is here
The bus fare is dear
But off we all trot
With costumes aloft
We change on the beach
Don't swim out of reach
Dear Mam will advise
As tides do arise
And when it comes in
We move farther off
And leave our sandcastles
Submerged by the froth.

THE FLIGHT OF STEPS

I dreamt a long awaited dream
To reach the stars, to fly with you
For every time I looked askance
Your image formed with every glance

The flight of steps was 'fore my eyes
And at the top the purple skies
A glow of radiance held my soul
I longed to reach that earthly goal

I toiled to climb and suddenly
Your caring hand reached out to me
And all at once I stood before
Your loving arms and open door

Beside you at the journey's end
I never left my dearest friend
For now my sight is growing dim
I feel the warmth of love within

We reach the end of Journey's time
The stars appear and you are mine
I'm filled with rapture as you care
And now at last I've reached that stair.

GLASGOW CITY

Do you remember Glasgow City?
Its rain drenched streets
And busy Central Station

Did you walk on Sauchiehall Street?
Peering in Pringle's window
Wanting to buy a tartan

Did you eat at Willow Tea Rooms?
Travelling by Open Top Bus
Viewing ancient buildings

Were you inspired by the Cathedral?
Sobered by the Necropolis
Challenged by Salvadore Dali

Did you love Rennie Mackintosh?
The house, the work, the designs
The roses, figures and furnishings

Wouldn't you love to go again?
To see the Clyde and shipping
The gardens and the people

Have a good and happy trip
A relaxing, great vacation
And if you're free, then meet with me
In the hub of Central Station.

BOOKMARKS

The book of my life fell open
And on the page I read
That this was where I met you
And this is what I said

A kind face, a gentle manner
A sweet and courteous man

A learned friend, supportive too
He'll hold you up in all you do
Discover him if you can

I marked the page with a bookmark
A little dog-ear too
So in later life, in times of strife
I'd look my friend to you

The book of my life fell open
To a present warm and sunny
We'd met and dined
We'd all but refined
A friendship sweet as honey

I marked the spot with a bookmark
A little dog-ear too
For this was the place
I loved your sweet face
So tell me what can I do?

The book of my life falls open
Before a future cold and bleak
For without you I'm lost
No end to this frost
I feel quite helpless and weak

I'll mark this place with a bookmark
A little dog-ear too
And once this is o'er
I'll love you the more
And hold you in all that you do

The book of my life will be closing
Eternity spreads before
I'll spend it with you

If you love me too
So open that final door

For now I've run out of bookmarks
And little dog-ears too
I miss your dear face
And in a short space
I hope that we'll see it through.

A PENTECOSTAL PRAYER FOR PROFIT

There's gloom on the High Street
Our profits are down
Three-for-two offers
Pervade the whole town

When shopping for food
Our stores display greed
Replacing their humans
With robots for speed

Bring back your carriers
Save lost energy
Save time if it's quicker
But don't worry me

Unwanted item
Remove it at once
Can't use the machine
You must be a dunce

In all this confusion
What would Jesus say
At the lack of good news

On the High Street today?

But hear the Apostles
Speak out words of love
Give service to others
Take heart from above

The spirit is with us
His words we adore
Show patience, grant kindness
Love others the more

The moment it takes
To give out a smile
May help your near neighbour
Go one extra mile

A second of thought
A word in your ear
Then I am transformed
And live without fear

Take heart every day
From Pentecost's story
Then reach out and share
In our Master's glory

We worship, we praise Him
We love Him the more
Remember when calling
At the High Street store.

THE MYSTERIOUS MONSTER OF MIDSOMER MADNESS

'Twas in the light of early June
When daylight lasted 'till the moon
Old Ronald did his garden grow
His voice was sweet, his limbs were slow

Amongst the Astro-meri-a
The Lupins and Lobelli-a
He spied the turd of a Monster grim
The terrible Midsomer Fiend within

The Monster grim lived in the ground
It weighed a mighty thousand pounds
It lived on grubs and fungal spores
And ooz-ed slime from every pore.

Old Ronald took his trusty fork
Went out one night all after dark
A cunning trap he did prepare
To catch the Monster in his lair

Ron had to wait until cock crow
The Monster's head began to show
It loomed large in the lamp glow
Then screamed, some Rotter's got my toe.

In vain did monstrous fiend leap forth
In vain it screamed for all it's worth
The trap did grip more tightly then
Old Ron put poison in the den.

Seeing the end so soon was nigh
Ron said, young fiend prepare to die

No more my garden will you mess
No more my Lupins will you press.

But fiendish though the Monster be
He gently went down on one knee
Oh kindly Ronald, dearest friend
Oh spare me, spare me from this end

Henceforth I swear I will be good
I'll never poo on your fresh food
Your Lupins will I leave alone
And always keep my turds at home.

From that day forth the loving pair
Would walk abroad to take the air
Firm friends in Ronald's garden bliss
You'd think they'd never been remiss.

ANSAPHONE

I'm here all alone in the hall
I'm fixed to this paint splattered wall
There's no one at home
I'm all on my own
I'm here in the dark, freezing hall.

A thrill runs through me at last
I can't move because I'm stuck fast
Oh please be for me
For who can it be?
I'm ringing the air with a blast.

Hi Barbara it's me, says a voice
I really have cause to rejoice

I've published my work, I never did shirk
I've made millions but feel such a Burk.
I've published my memoirs, you see,
And now half the world's suing me
I've told all the tales, spread lies throughout Wales
Now family and friends, to make their own ends
Are going to Court, I need bail.

Oh Barbara please phone back at once,
Please say I'm not really a dunce
I've caused such a palaver, I'm in such a lather
Oh help if you will, it's a witch hunt.

Then silence pervades the air
She's hung up and I breathe a sigh
Oh how can it be, it's never for me?
If only someone would say why?

Then suddenly a tring once again
Oh who is it now? I feel pain,
Hello Barbara, the Minister's here,
Our action is really quite clear
It seems your dear daughter
Ain't done what she oughta
We have to expel her from here.

I breathe a big sigh of relief
But really I'm racked by my grief
For when there's a call, I sit on my wall
And take all the bad news each week.

Then once again I am ringing
Then at last my heart starts singing
For a sweet, gentle voice says,
You have no choice,
You're an ansaphone fixed to the wall

You're really innocuous and small
But each time I hear you I know that you give me
Much opportunity way beyond the wall.

You lend an ear to good things and bad,
Pass messages happy and sad,
And each time I ring, you do your great thing
And everybody is glad.

So hear me speak up for the 'phone
Don't ignore me, hang up or moan
It's really quite clear, you know why I'm here
'Cos Barbara and Peter aren't home.

H2O

Revolving in an endless shift
The molecules spin, their parts adrift
Yet order stems from every part
A living stream as neutrons dart

I pour the water, H2O
With scarce a thought for all that flow
I drink it down, I bathe, I swim
I take it up and soak it in

But oft' I gaze out far to sea
Lost in rapture and rhapsody
I hear the water lash the shore
Singing out to its melody

With every different kind of form
A river deep, a summer storm
This mighty molecule takes its shape

From earthly bonds, divinely made

No wonder crafted in this world
Can e're compare to water's swirl
Drink deep my friend and pass the cup
Let's celebrate, with joyous cup.

A Boy's Anthem

A BEAUTIFUL GAME

I thought I'd buy a soccer team
To teach my son to play,
We'd practise in the local park
And play 'till break of day
I put a freebie advert
Upon the Internet
And soon a football manager
Rang up to charge me rent
The team was Tuff United
At prices very high
I set the bidding promptly
But soon they reached the sky.
The greatest football player
I managed to procure
He took my son for lessons
Then asked for even more.
Politely I rejoindered
Young Sam had had enough
And maybe Mr. Soccer
Could return to play with Tuff.
At last he went and left us
To play instead at Lords
For cricket at its embers
Brought greater life rewards.

A SEAGULL'S SONG

This rooftop ledge is now my home

A perilous, windy place to be
With lashing rain and blazing sun
A substitute for rock and scree

I came here many moons ago
My forebears would not want to see
A change of life so out of sorts
With what my Nature says should be

But with a shrug I make the best
And here I build my urban nest
My brood is small, but hear my call
From dawn to dusk I take no rest

Mankind is not my normal friend
We often fight to different ends
It cannot be what God intends
That I should feed on streetside shreds

My chicks are hatching, soon I'll be
A menace as I swoop and dive
An instinct to protect, survive
Means I will take what's left for me

So as my shrill and strident cry
Resounds throughout this City's sky
Preserve my fishing rights at sea
Or else a pest I'll always be.

AS PETALS FALL

The rose bud, tight and green
Holds promise, firmly clenched against
The elements still raging as winter

Gives way to latent spring

Movement, hardly noticed, almost still
Yet checked by nothing
Late frost, harsh rain
The bud stands firm as colour shows again

A hint of red, and as it opens
Its fellows join the floral chorus
Suddenly a bloom most perfect
The transition like a miracle
A gift of Nature's art

The rose, like wine or pigments deep
Fills the air with fragrance
A rhapsody complete
Such matchless symmetry
And soft enchanting poetry

Time will pass, the year moves on
The petals fade and fall
My pledge to you, as I grow old
To gather roses by your side
Forever at your call.

IMMORTALITY

Dad, will I grow to be like you?
What, grumpy, balding, false teeth too?
No Daddy hero of my dreams
A man of substance, on whom I lean.
Well son, a story I will tell
Of how I did turn out so well
A tale of striving, caring love

As told by angels from above

One day I walked to work at four
Unlocked the foreman's canteen door
Beheld a vision, lovely, thought
I'll marry her, she's a good sport

The foreman came with pick axe aloft
I see you've met my wife he quaffed
Bad luck for me I figured quashed
But soon I met her sister Chloe
And she it was advised me so

If you my husband brave would be
Work hard, don't shirk and be prepared
To live a life of grace with ease
And other women never tease

Be courteous, patient, and I'll show
Unswerving devotion every day
And this, my son is why you're here
But my last word is be of cheer

They'll tell you it's a certain thing
That Dad will leave you follow him
But you don't need to die his death
Just love, adore your lady wife

We're not immortal, none can be
But follow through your Family Tree
Leave kindness in perpetuity
For then you will remembered be.

RADIANT FIRE AND TRANSLUCENT FLAME

As each tongue of flaming fire
Leapt from edge to edge
As sounds emerged on wings of song
I saw without all doubt my heart
Expand with new and living love
As certain time was born above

An angel spoke and from his lips
More beauty than I've ever known
A tale so good of truth and valour
To stir my soul with notes so sweet
I'm moved beyond all earthly bounds
And sing with cherubs joy to greet

Did you not hear the angel song?
The heavenly chorus and mighty throng
Ah blissful peace, the sounds it soothes
The senses gripped, the voices prove
That here was dreaming come to find
A more secure and lasting mind
I've found what I was searching for
A place to rest, with opening door.

WITH GOLDEN GLOW

Sunrise kissed a rain drenched earth
Chrysanthemums of gold
Were tinged with shades of day and night
For love that had gone cold

The drops of water glistening shone
I wiped them from my brow

Arriving home I fetched the bowl
To place the flowers therein

When darkness fell, no love returned
No welcome, tender kiss
My soul in pain I wept alas
With morning came a brighter hope
The flowers still a vibrant glow
My hands picked up the telephone
And longed for love I called

It's you he cried, where have you been?
I waited half a year
I thought I'd never hear again
I've sold your favourite chair!

Oh darling muse, no faith you have
A tearful sob I cried
For if I left e'en a week
My spirit just would die.

So Christmas came and muse and I
To Panto had recourse
The golden glow of Elf Queen's robe
Was yellow as the sun at noon
So we ate popcorn with a spoon!

EVERGREEN

Live for autumn, green for spring
I sport my berries as carollers sing
No death awaits my prickly sting
I am eternally fresh, as wings
Of swallows leave the North

Heading for a basking sun
Since birds could fly
And seasons run

I witnessed life and death that day
His body cold and wasted lay
His mother knelt in earnest prayer
It seemed no hope remained for her
Yet later at a count of three
He rose in triumph for all to see
So surely then as sages tell
The Holly Bush was green and yet

My greatest fear is fire and flood
Extinguishing my very blood
But see the landscape afterward
The sap returns, the life renewed
A voice of hope cries out to me
See! See! The Lord has sent a dove

So with the New Year rushing in
I'm swept aside like forgiven sin
My branches lie discarded now
But in a year, my berries show.

IN PERFECT HARMONY

Walk with me through dark and stony places
Share with me the light of happy days
Talk about the love that lies between us
Though hard our path, and thorny all our ways

The truest spirit quails at dark of evening
While bravest souls despair when night is long

But with the dawn new hope can now inspire us
As rapture greets the sound of morning song.

For many dangers lure imagination
Our fears seem rational, looming large and grim
Until we sleep away our wildest worries
Rejoicing as we put our trust in Him.

Walk with me through pleasant times and sadness
Stay with me as I grow old and wise
Our lives will yield a share of perfect gladness
In harmony with the Lord of earth and skies.

MY GIFT TO YOU

I have a little time to spare
A moment's thought to show I care
So here today I give to you
An hour a week, a lifetime's through

I cannot promise that I'll be
Always even tempered, serene
But every time I see you this
I hope our lives will surely cross

To give each other and the world
More business and more joys unfurled
We keep in touch by wire and word
Promoting human good by turns

If you should call me up one day
To ask can I be free to pay?
My due is at your sole command
I'm free of heart and free of hand

It sounds an idle boast to some
But only speak and I will come
Your every need must surely be
A greater richness called from me.

I have a little time to spare
Each moment precious, brief and rare
Live every second to its last
Hold all our memories close and fast.

REVERSI

Sweet summer sun shines on, shines on
I lie without a care
The skylarks sing, the church bells ring
Grass grows, leaves hardly stir
A bee disturbs my slumber soft
Searching for food
Reaching for mead
To make honey every year
Far and away the farmyard stirs
A visitor proclaimed
Come Jenny leave your musings thus
Come harvest before it rains
Threshing, mowing, moving chaff
The rhythm of our days
With hardly a variation
Of earth's timely rotation
Shine on, shine on, cool orb of night
The moon beams down
The world's all right.

THE ELF KING'S DREAM

With eyelids dropt the Elf King slept
But trouble stirred his soul
He tossed and turned, his spirit yearned
To find his silver bowl

The magic bowl was used by all
To make a wish come true
But horrid Mr Just Don't Care
Had put the bowl inside his lair
And no-one knew exactly where

The Elf King dreamed a dream that night
That fairies came his way
They spoke of all his Elf Land's plight
That must at once be put aright
So peace could reign for evermore
But trouble first must close its door.

When morning broke and sunshine came
The Elf King left with Queen Lorraine
And all his guards and royal train
To seek the lair of dark despair
Where lurked the lonely Just Don't Care

Come out my friend, please have no fear
We only come to bring you cheer
The silver bowl you have in there
Is worthless lest you are insured

The fearsome Mr Just Don't Care
Leapt out at once and punched the air
It's worth a mint and I am skint
But I will give you half an hour

To help my daughter who is ill
Then I'll repay whate'er you will

The daughter came before the King
Who gently knelt and said please miss
If you my son would only kiss
The world would be a better place.

Well soon the pair were married off
And Elfin Queen begs do not scoff
It's love that makes the world go round
But decent sleep is treasure sound.

WATERS MEET

Straight from its source the river flows
I wonder how or where?
A stream that ever quickly grows
To meet its fellow here

I know not who dictates its wrath
In flood or furious storm
I only know at times of peace
Its life gives health to all

I've often sat at this dear place
Just gazing o'er the meads
A stillness, softness soon descends
With sweet tranquillity

The swans have cygnets, ducks their young
Lambs suckle, butterflies in flight
No time exists, just cycling through
Diurnal rhythms daily made

An endless day and night

I would return throughout the year
To see the swans progress
Until such time I'm called away
Departing on the later train
Wreathed in sunshine, blessed by rain.

THE PEN PIXIE

My name is Snaffle Chops
I come from far away
I live behind the skirting board
And while my life is free
I have a naughty habit
You'll never pin on me

I take the ballpoint biros
I am a crafty thief
I hide where you can't see me
But always get my meat

I thrive and thrive on ball points
You'll live to rue the day
You left your ball point resting
Where I can snatch and play

Yes I'm the biro pixie
I'll steal them one and all
The more you buy, I'll be close by
And munch 'till they are gone

My friends they call me ink spot
But Snaffle Chops is my name

I'm sorry to admit it
But your ball point's gone again.

CENTENARY

Daddy tell me if you please
Of one hundred years ago
About how Grandad fought in vain
Upon a foreign shore

We'll son, it's not a source of pride
No joy or pleasure comes
But war is still a constant threat
For generations to come

The military equipment
Sophisticated grows
And still in these enlightened times
Mankind makes bitter foes

But there's a hope we all can win
A triumph that prevailed
When our dear Lord was crucified
Our lives were surely saved

He died for one, He died for all
And three days later rose
So to His glory we must try
To eradicate our woes

Remember son that Grandad's war
Did not end fighting then
So turn your spears to pruning hooks
And love your fellow men.

FEEL THE PULSE

Nurse my pulse is soaring
The streets are paved with gold
A flowing of my bloodstream
To coincide with all
That makes us as a nation
Unite with one accord
And share our jubilations
One voice, one mind, one chord.

For lo the time is coming
When we will all be free
With rapture in our calling
In joyous psalmody.

The journey may be taxing
Our hearts oft' prone to doubt
But working with our neighbours
Must put the world aright

So brother, sister, comrade
Throw down your arms today
Show peaceful, tranquil targets
And lead those gone astray

If Heaven is our goal post
The Lord our holy guide
Let's link our arms together
In strength and side by side.

Dear Nurse I feel more calm now
Sweet rest is close at hand

My daily work is over
There's peace throughout the Land.

THE GUNS WERE STILLED

The papers say, the papers say
That shelling ceased upon that day
That Victory was won indeed
For those in Europe, still in need

The aftermath we'll deal with now
Complete surrender was their vow
Our lives will never be the same
The horror leaves its mark in graves

Their row on row of grisly tale
Our grandsons honour every day
They gave their lives and we must know
That freedom was so dearly bought.

Let's not forget as time will heal
The courage, camaraderie and peals
Of bells will ring out now
Our solace after time of war

His sorrow we must surely feel
The Lord must not have died in vain
So look ahead to feel the breach
Make reparation as He did teach.

ON COVENTRY CATHEDRAL

The ancient walls of St Michael's church

Stand firm for all to see
A testament to the power of God
In all this misery

The centre hollowed by a bomb
The inscription simply reads
"Father forgive", is all it says
For all our sins redeemed

The new Cathedral, brick by brick
Was built of glass and stone
The view right through the great West doors
With etchings sharp and endless light
Brings sun and daylight to long held nights.

This is proof, if proof were needed
That humanity's ills may be superseded
That our new build shows strength of will
For with the love of God instilled
Some kindness, care and determination
Here's a message to all nations.

The fighting's ceased, the build began
A thing of beauty, that always can
Lead, inspire and show the way
For this is our most radiant day.

FLIGHTS OF FANCY

I'd love to sail the ocean
Or travel to the Moon
If only I could fly sky high
In my hot air balloon

My fate is fairly humdrum
An office is my lot
But in my dreams the welcome mat
Provides a magic carpet, that
Takes me out of bounds.

I'm off to Scandinavia
I fly to Kazakhstan
Then Junior down the corridor
Cries Sir can you please sign?

I'm signing others papers
Fulfilling the public's dream
To race through snow in Russia
Or paint the church at Rheims.

Yes I'm an operator
Of tours and travel tales
And one day soon I'll journey far
Away from wintery Wales.

I'll see the peaks of Prussia
The woods of Germany
I'll jump aboard the train line
Composing symphonies

But back here at the office
Young Junior's gone to tea
I'll sign these travel papers
Whilst gazing out to sea.

SWEET MAYTIME

Sunrise, blue at ease with pink
A gentle shower moves swiftly on
And all at once a thousand tongues
Give voice to undulating song.

Hear the skylark soaring, calling
Was a cuckoo distinctly heard?
Blossoms tinged with dewdrops opening
Hawthorn flower in cream displaying
Perfume sweet as any worn.

Come friend with me to gather garlands
Cross the fields as shines the sun
Pin them o'er the oak beams standing
Firm affixed above the door.

But let not those branches inside
Or ill luck will be thy fate
For the scent of May time garlands
Could resemble death's dark date.

Here am I at journey's ending
Precious life ebbs softly by
Sweet the flower that marks our passing
Blossoms fill celestial skies.

Trumpets sound with angels greeting
Joyous fine cacophony
At last the hour, the day, the dawning
Cymbals clash in rhapsody.

BLUEBELL WOODS

Waking sounds of city streets
Draw my mind to thoughts of home
Back to times of springtime pleasure
When with you my footsteps roamed.

Leaving pavements hard, unyielding
Feeling grass beneath our feet
Hand in hand we both would wander
Seeking out a floral retreat.

First the comely celandine
Yellow as the sun at noon
Joined with primrose, pale and pretty
Then the violets white and blue.

Later on a bluebell carpet
Mass on mass of scented blooms
Thick the stems beneath the branches
Then the red tinged, yellow broom.

For this joy is never ceasing
A source of wonder every year
But thinking back to scenes of childhood
I would often shed a tear.

Cares and worries all forgotten
See the faded photographs
Wasn't Uncle Charley handsome?
Well remembered his throaty laugh.

Re-awakened city noises
Recall my mind to present self
I must go in search of bluebells

Rich and heady, who needs wealth?

BOWLS NIGHT

We're all convinced, with one accord
The floor has got a kink
I bowled it straight, I bowled it true
I didn't even blink.

But see the wood has gone astray
And now the reds are in the lead
So I will hope my game improves
With tea and biscuits afterwards.

We'll see, the younger wood replied
My odd behaviour mystifies
I have a mind, a will, a soul
For even though you give your all
If I am feeling so inclined
I'll leap about right off the side.

It's not a life I'd call my own
To roll on carpet and be thrown
To hurl myself right down the room
But boy it's fun to spoil the game.

Alright for some said Mr Jack
At least you journey forth and back
I sit alone and rarely move
Until I'm smacked as if reproved.

Don't moan at me the carpet cried
I'm squashed at night and stored inside
Then placed upon a wooden floor

And bowled all over, more and more.

So wood with Jack and rug unite
We'll get them if we have to fight
For we decide the game's dark fate
If score you must, you'll have to wait.

The most skilled players make mistakes
But we the woods must stay awake
And just as night is drawing in
We never see the biscuit tin.

A strike is called for said the wood
But loyal carpet wants to be good
For after all it's harmless fun
And now at least the reds have won.

SWEET CONSOLATION

Dear delight, sweet consolation
Cause for hearty celebration
Darker days and longer nights
Colder weather, snowflakes bright
Time for bouts of comfort eating
Chocolate, cake is pleasure fleeting
But when sunshine stays away
Take a bite to warm the day.

Heat the water, mash the tea
Come and spend an hour with me
Two can dine in winter splendour
Safe indoors beside the fender
Roasted chestnuts, baked marshmallows
All the treats that we can swallow

Dear delight, sweet consolation
Cause for hearty celebration.

Finish with a slice of cheese
Pass the pepper if you please
Crack the nuts and peel the fruit
Chop the carrots, chew the shoots
Make we merry with some wine
Mulling spices old as time
Dear delight sweet consolation
Cause for hearty celebration.

LINE'S FOR ST FAITH'S CHAPEL, WESTMINSTER ABBEY

Dear Lord, here in this place
Where I first found your love
Keep me safe from harm this night
Teach me from above
Lead me in your ways of mercy
May I never fail
Show the care my Master taught me
Let your strength prevail
Keep my mind on thoughts of courage
Save me from all doubt
Cast aside my weary burden
Bestow your gentle light
For my soul your consolation
Guides me through each day
Ever loving Holy Father
May I heed your ways
If the time comes when I meet you
Help me through that door
Father, Son and Holy Spirit

Now and evermore.

THE VOLUNTEER

Hide not your light beneath a bushel
Shine forth to all with radiance aglow
Smile as you glide behind pillars you hide
Reveal your kind face in this magic place
Guide us and lead us to altar to feed us
Oh Warden of Bath!

Spread sparkle at Christmas to millions unknown
Show comfort to others bereft and alone
Wear your badge with pride, direct us from one side
Stride over dale, stay hearty and hale
Oh Warden of Bath!

May driving vacations fill family with cheer
The lovely assistant says this in your ear
It's left at the turning, you'll have to go back
Watch out for those children - no, don't take the track.
To work with each other is surely a skill
A proof of commitment, good works and good will,
Oh Warden of Bath!

To end this fair ditty I simply will add
That all our church members are really quite glad
That our volunteers are part of the fabric
As much as the stone, the glass and the brick
The bells and the feasting
The fasting, the pews, the bread and the wine
Oh Warden of Bath!

FLORIBUNDA IN THE MORNING

My forebears would be very happy to help you with the issues that affect your ability to work. In the morning room of the new acceptance letter, to the wheel of fortune from the Kennet and Avon Canal, Greetings and a vast experience of empowering adults to achieve satisfaction and fulfilment of the new acceptance recently sold. Flowers for Algernon and a cake slice of pizza hut, to be abolished and the world library.

I am not sure if you have received this communication in the past few years, now and then we will put you on Monday morning here, and there was temporary work. Onward transmission opening or using any different ends up being made to order the appraisal is the possibility that I can receive them.

Today we are looking forward to receiving your response and I will be travelling with you Sir. Tomorrow I have been friends since the beginning by asking how Sir Arnold is looking forward to seeing everyone.

Inspired by Mozart's Musical Joke, the above letter was written using the prompts from my Tablet as I progressed. I have added three words and randomly inserted punctuation - see if you can guess which words they are. The title of this silly piece is FLORIBUNDA from a name I bestowed upon my friend's great granddaughter.